T0286947

Cambridge Elements ≡

Elements in Environmental Humanities
edited by
Louise Westling
University of Oregon
Serenella Iovino
University of North Carolina at Chapel Hill
Timo Maran
University of Tartu

INDIGENOUS KNOWLEDGE AND MATERIAL HISTORIES

The Example of Rubber

Jens Soentgen
Augsburg University

CAMBRIDGE
UNIVERSITY PRESS

Shaftesbury Road, Cambridge CB2 8EA, United Kingdom

One Liberty Plaza, 20th Floor, New York, NY 10006, USA

477 Williamstown Road, Port Melbourne, VIC 3207, Australia

314–321, 3rd Floor, Plot 3, Splendor Forum, Jasola District Centre,
New Delhi – 110025, India

103 Penang Road, #05–06/07, Visioncrest Commercial, Singapore 238467

Cambridge University Press is part of Cambridge University Press & Assessment,
a department of the University of Cambridge.

We share the University's mission to contribute to society through the pursuit of
education, learning and research at the highest international levels of excellence.

www.cambridge.org
Information on this title: www.cambridge.org/9781009517089

DOI: 10.1017/9781009442756

© Jens Soentgen 2024

This publication is in copyright. Subject to statutory exception and to the provisions of
relevant collective licensing agreements, no reproduction of any part may take place
without the written permission of Cambridge University Press & Assessment.

When citing this work, please include a reference to the DOI 10.1017/9781009442756

First published 2024

A catalogue record for this publication is available from the British Library.

ISBN 978-1-009-51708-9 Hardback
ISBN 978-1-009-44272-5 Paperback
ISSN 2632-3125 (online)
ISSN 2632-3117 (print)

Cambridge University Press & Assessment has no responsibility for the persistence
or accuracy of URLs for external or third-party internet websites referred to in this
publication and does not guarantee that any content on such websites is, or will
remain, accurate or appropriate.

Indigenous Knowledge and Material Histories

The Example of Rubber

Elements in Environmental Humanities

DOI: 10.1017/9781009442756
First published online: May 2024

Jens Soentgen
Augsburg University
Author for correspondence: Jens Soentgen, soentgen@wzu.uni-augsburg.de

Abstract: This Element deals with stories about substances and ways to analyze them through an environmental humanities perspective. It takes rubber and its many stories as an example. It argues that common notions of rubber history, which assume that rubber only became a useful material through a miraculous chemical operation called vulcanization, attributed to the US-American Charles Goodyear, are false. In contrast, the Element demonstrates that rubber and many important rubber products are the inventions of Indigenous peoples of South America, made durable by a process that can be called organic vulcanization. It is with that invention that the story of rubber starts. Without it, rubber would not exist, neither in the Americas nor elsewhere. Finally, it is shown that Indigenous rubber products offer some ecological advantages over industrially manufactured ones.

Keywords: Indigenous knowledge, Indigenous chemistry, postcolonial perspectives, material histories, rubber

© Jens Soentgen 2024

ISBNs: 9781009517089 (HB), 9781009442725 (PB), 9781009442756 (OC)
ISSNs: 2632-3125 (online), 2632-3117 (print)

Contents

1 Introduction   1

2 The Rhetorical and Literary Tradition of Stories of Stuff   4

3 Research on the History of Individual Substances   14

4 Substances and Materials   18

5 Histories and Stories   24

6 The Origins of Rubber   30

7 Rubber Histories and the Representation of Indigenous Peoples of South and Central America   35

8 Indigenous Knowledge   40

9 Indigenous Rubber Products   43

10 Problems of Untreated Rubber   45

11 The Place of Indigenous Knowledge in the History of Rubber   50

12 Rubber and Rubbish: Tire Dumps and Microrubber   52

References   57

1 Introduction

Aside from things such as smartphones, keyboards, bookshelves, tables and chairs, our environment includes substances. Such substances are not only present in material things. We often come into contact with them directly, such as when we work with flour, sugar, water, and milk in the kitchen, for example, or when we spread butter on bread. A substance is therefore not only something we know indirectly. Nor do we need the natural sciences, such as chemistry, to get to know substances; we come into direct contact with them in our everyday lives. This is not only a philosophical opinion; it is also shown in psychological studies of perception (Gibson, 1979).

There are essentially two ways in which we get to know substances. First, we handle them. A child gets to know sand by playing with it, letting it run through their fingers, or wetting it with water and then making "sandcakes" out of it. Other types of materials are also explored directly by children, not always to the enthusiasm of their parents. Directly handling substances is something we do throughout our lives, such as when learning to melt chocolate or when preparing cake dough.

But we also get to know substances in a second way, namely, by hearing about them. We "know" them by hearsay. This means that we hear stories about substances while we are getting to know them, and this is often before we come into contact with them directly. These stories tell us what specific substances are all about, what they look like, what kind of behavior they have, or even what we can do with them and where they come from.

One could regard such stories as precursors of true knowledge, but in very many cases we get to know substances *only* through stories. For example, very few people have ever *consciously* come into contact with carbon dioxide or ozone, and yet most have heard and read stories about these substances. In fact, one could make the case that a great many, perhaps even the majority, of all the substances that people somehow have contact with are conveyed through stories. This holds true, for example, for almost all so-called pollutants, that is, substances that may be present in tiny residues in food or that may be found in traces in textiles or children's toys. Very few people know about such substances based on their own direct experience.

This also applies to the many supposedly unproblematic materials that make up the electronic devices we use every day. Very few of them are really known to the people who use these devices. But we read and hear about them all the time. We hear that a smartphone contains around sixty different materials (Reller et al., 2009), and among them thirty metals, but of this diversity we actually know of maybe only gold and copper. Who knows anything about neodymium, indium, tantalum, dysprosium, or gadolinium? And yet all of these substances are contained in every smartphone. Textiles are also no longer only made of "cotton" or "nettle," but are made out of synthetic polymers that have been treated with dye, coatings, and other synthetic materials.

Often, what we learn about the substances in our environment has the character of information in which a single, isolated fact is communicated to us. For example, you may read in the newspaper that every smartphone contains a whole series of rare metals. You then learn a fact and receive a piece of information.

Many times, however, such information is conveyed in the context of stories. You may read on the internet or in a newspaper's headlines that a certain famous brand of mineral water has been "contaminated," "laced," or "tainted" with benzene. When you then read that benzene is a "component of crude oil" that is "cancer-causing" and a "flammable poison," you are definitely no longer reading neutral information, but rather an emotionalized story in which a tremendous threat has suddenly appeared where you had least expected it, namely, in expensive bottles of mineral water that are, or at least were, supposed to contain only the purest and most innocent substance from nature (Schwarz, 2019).

Such stories may interest people because they are relevant to their health, but often the context is broader. We might read about climate change, for example, that it is supposed to be one of the greatest threats to the continuation of civilized human life on the planet. Yet this apocalyptic, dystopian frame is at the same time a story about a certain substance. Climate change is, after all, driven by carbon dioxide in the atmosphere.

In sum, very often, we learn about substances from the media in the context of stories. This is not just the case today. The history of ozone, for example, shows that already in the nineteenth century people did not handle this substance directly, but rather read about it. Our ancestors learned about this newly discovered substance not from firsthand experience but from newspapers and magazines. And what they read certainly influenced their behavior, since it was believed at the time that ozone was beneficial to health. People literally sought out places where it was particularly concentrated and tried to inhale as much as they could. Such articles and the stories they contained about ozone were usually short (Zemanek, 2023). Even today many people learn most of the things they know about this or that substance from the TV, the internet and other electronic media, or from newspapers and magazines.

And new forms of communication about substances have also surfaced. Entire books and novels about substances were published in the twentieth century. I will refer to them mostly as "material stories or histories," although I sometimes call them substance stories or stories of stuff (approximating the German term

"Stoffgeschichten"). I will not be too rigid in the designation; however, I will be very eager to show examples and analyze them in order to make clear what I mean. Anyway, these material histories soon became an established part of the genre of literary nonfiction. Today, not a book fair goes by without the presentation of new works of this kind, some of them even meeting high literary standards. One can speak of a nonfiction genre of its own in the case of these biographies of materials. One can delve into the ocean of this or that substance, immerse in its stories.

Such books have become commonplace; they are widely read. In 2005, for example, a book about salt was on the summer reading list of then US president, George W. Bush. The general interest in stories about substances is not surprising, however, when one considers the extent to which substances of all kinds are mobilized by modern society (Smil, 2013, see also Soentgen, 2023) – and how great the dependence on them has become. Although some of our technical devices are becoming smaller and more manageable, which might result in less consumption of material resources, overall the demand for raw materials, across almost all substances, is increasing. This leads not only to problems of supply but also to other problems, such as where we put the things we no longer need. As we use more and more substances and materials, which are in many cases traded around the world, the mountains of garbage on land, and the garbage vortices in the ocean are growing. The total weight of plastic produced by humans since the 1950s now exceeds the mass of all animals on land and in water (Geyer et al., 2017). If you think about this figure and look more closely at modern Anthropocene research (Antweiler, 2022), you tend to wonder, not about the occurrence of such strange books on substances in book stores, but rather why there are not many more stories being told about substances. In any case, such stories do exist and they have considerable significance not only for our understanding but also for the practical, technical, and political treatment of substances.

These stories should therefore not only be collected but also studied, and the environmental humanities are well equipped to do this. They have developed sophisticated methods for analyzing stories, including stories about substances. This Element will analyze the traditions and perspectives that form part of material histories in general and then, as an example, look at the stories and histories associated with rubber.

Why rubber? Rubber may not tell "everything to everybody," as carbon does, at least according to Primo Levi (1975, p. 230), but it tells us a lot of things. It is well-known to virtually everybody, present at all age levels; children play with rubber toys and are fascinated by this material. In all areas of modern society, from space shuttles to manufacturing, from sex shops to intensive care units, and from children's playrooms to hiking stores, you will encounter rubber. For most of us, not a day goes by without touching rubber, using rubber, working with rubber; it is a ubiquitous part of contemporary life. Nevertheless, it has not always been with us. Rubber is a rather novel material. It was unknown to the "Old World" before the voyages of Christopher Columbus. Columbus and his crew were the first non-American people to encounter rubber. They saw rubber balls on Columbus' second voyage in 1496 and took some of them back to Seville. The balls' elasticity seemed to be a miracle. In nearly all early writings about the "New World," rubber was mentioned. However, we know very little about the fate of the first rubber items that were brought to Europe. None of them were conserved. Maybe children found them in the arsenals and played with them until they finally plopped into the Guadalquivir, the river that crosses the town of Seville and that might have transported them back to the Atlantic. Some Indigenous rubber products were traded in the eighteenth century, but the industrial use of rubber did not start until the nineteenth century.

Whole novels have been written about rubber, and new ones are still being written today. From the first encounter with rubber, this very material inspired stories. As rubber came originally from South America, it is not only a global but also a specifically transatlantic substance. In fact, I will argue that it can be considered one of the first of many important contributions that Indigenous people have made to contemporary material culture. The role that Indigenous people play in popular stories of rubber, as well as in scientific histories, is therefore particularly interesting.

Rubber, and the stories that are told about it and its invention, is my example of what one might call a "substance story," a "material history" or a "story of stuff." From a literary perspective, such stories seem rather strange and unusual, even though they can look back at a long tradition" oder "strange and unusual, as the next chapter will outline.

2 The Rhetorical and Literary Tradition of Stories of Stuff

Substance stories, have unusual heroes. Normally, stories are told about *people*, their fates, their adventures, their entanglements, and their achievements. Often it is extraordinary people or, at least, extraordinary events that are worth telling stories about.

Substances, however, are not normal heroes of stories. It is hard to create inquisitiveness about them and their behavior. All chemistry teachers know how difficult it is to generate interest in substances. Substances like sugar, salt, or coffee are well-known since they are used and consumed in everyday life. But aside from ecologists and chemists, who really wants to know more about substances than their price and their quality?

Or, to put it in a more optimistic way: What methods can be used to tell a captivating story about a given substance? This question is older than one might think. In fact, even in ancient rhetoric there are repeated references to orators who spoke not only about heroes, battles, and empires or about gold and silver – that would seem reasonable – but also about neglected and even disgusting substances like dust, smoke, excrement, and ashes. For example, Augustine of Hippo, who was a trained orator, mentions in his work *De vera religione* that one could very well sing the praises of ashes or even excrement without having to lie (Augustinus, 1962, p. 237). In fact, not only were there speeches on such substances, there were also quite sophisticated reflections on the aims and methods of such speeches. They seem to have played a distinctive role in the system of classical rhetoric.

Such stories appeared as *enkomia paradoxa* or paradoxical eulogies in ancient rhetoric. They were a special form of eulogy which enjoyed great popularity, especially in the so-called *Second Sophistic*. The *Second Sophistic* is a term used to describe a cultural period in the Imperium Romanum, which is usually narrowed down to between AD 60 and 230. During this period, but also before and after, paradoxical panegyrics were particularly popular. What were they about? Normal eulogies had to do with the deeds of important people, usually men and usually rulers. Gods or demigods as well as certain virtues were praised. In addition to these well-known types of speeches, the rhetoric of which was explained in almost all standard works of ancient rhetoric, eulogies were also delivered about inconspicuous and unworthy objects – for example, annoying insects such as flies. And not only flies, but also disgusting or at least less-respected substances were discussed. Often this kind of paradoxical eulogy was recommended as a teaching exercise to train the orator to be able to make a great speech, even about the smallest of things that supposedly yielded nothing. Thus, in public appearances or even in publications, orators praised inconspicuous substances such as dust or smoke (and not the emperor or Hercules).

As important as the genre seems to have been in rhetorical practice, especially in the imperial period, only one detailed description of how to compose such eulogies has survived. This was written by Marcus Cornelius Fronto (AD 100–170), a famous Roman grammarian and orator, who was also the tutor of the later emperor Marcus Aurelius. In a letter to Marcus Aurelius, written around AD 139, Fronto teaches:

> The topic, however, must everywhere be treated as if it were an important and splendid one, and trifling things must be likened and compared to great ones. Finally, the highest merit in this kind of discourse is an attitude of seriousness. Tales of gods or men must be brought in where appropriate; so, too, pertinent

verses and proverbs that are applicable, and ingenious fictions, provided that
the fiction is helped out by some witty reasoning. (Haines, 1919, pp. 41–43)

Following this recipe, Fronto then formulates a eulogy on dust and smoke,
which has only survived in very fragmentary form. Nevertheless, one can
immediately see that he sticks to his own formula. For he addresses both
substances as gods: "I will therefore praise gods who are indeed not much in
evidence in the matter of praises, but are very much in evidence in the experience and life of men, Smoke and Dust, without whom neither altars, nor hearths,
nor highways, as people say, nor paths can be used" (Haines, 1919, p. 45). He
then adds the reflection that it is surely a characteristic of the divine nature of
smoke that it, like the gods themselves, cannot be grasped with one's hands. Yet
the rest of the eulogy, especially the sections on dust, have not survived. The
rather short and only partially surviving letter, which was presumably written in
the year in which Marcus Aurelius was appointed Caesar and thus established
by his adoptive father Antoninus Pius as the later heir to the throne, is nevertheless exceedingly revealing. It emphasizes that speeches of this kind served,
above all, to entertain. Therefore, the stylistic feature of *suavitas*, sweetness,
was also a characteristic of such speeches: they should be sweet like a mild
wine. And Fronto, both through his reflections and examples, gives indications
on how to proceed in achieving this: mythological embellishments are important, as well as poetic quotations. But imagination also plays a role. To emphasize the importance of annoying everyday companions like dust and smoke,
Fronto enumerates all the things that would not exist without them. All of these
techniques also appear in contemporary novels and stories on substances.

In the Renaissance, this kind of eulogy was cultivated again (Billerbeck &
Zubler, 2000, pp. 1–53, see also Tomarken, 1990). Johannes Kepler, for
example, wrote an extensive treatise on snow, which he dedicated to his friend
Johannes Wacker von Wackenfels. This work on a well-known but little appreciated substance stands clearly in the tradition of paradoxical eulogies. The
point, for Kepler, was to present something that seemingly cannot be
a meaningful subject for a text, but that is nevertheless treated in detail and
with much perspicacity. The special joke in this writing lies in the fact that snow
in Latin is "nix." As Kepler expressly points out, this word is synonymous with
"nothing" in colloquial German. The work thus ironically plays with this double
meaning – it is a treatise about nothing at all.

The paradoxical eulogies by no means schematically applied praise to such
unfamiliar objects, but rather depicted these objects quite accurately. In this
sense, snow is not only praised, but at the same time scientifically explored in
these writings, with Kepler highlighting, in particular, the hexagonal shape of

snow crystals (Kepler, 1611). His writings about snow are therefore still being discussed today in the history of science, not least because of a famous mathematical conjecture that was first published in this text.

Humanist writers also liked to write about insects, such as flies and fleas, as well as about diseases and vices such as carelessness and stupidity, alongside other topics that were usually either despised or went unnoticed. While the paradoxical eulogies of the Renaissance are well studied, the survival of the genre in Baroque literature has so far, to my knowledge, not been well researched.

The paradoxical eulogies were always short. In the eighteenth century, however, regular novels dealing with inanimate objects appeared for the first time. In literary studies they are called *It-narratives* (also *novels of circulation*); they are narratives whose hero is a thing, such as a gold coin, a corkscrew, a silver spoon, a coat, or even an atom (Douglas, 1995, pp. 130–161, also Soentgen, 2014 and Blackwell, 2007). The narrative unfolds from the perspective of these objects on the people and events around them. Here, then, a supposedly inanimate thing is taken as offering a perspective, but it is not a static object as it has a mobile vantage point. It is used as a kind of spy (Festa, 2015), which can inconspicuously observe from blind angles, thus having access to otherwise little-known or even hidden places and events. These narratives are therefore about the odyssey of these objects through the human world. Such novels were especially popular in the British Empire of the eighteenth century and reflect the increasing amount of goods that were traded and circulated throughout the Empire. They reflected a changed relationship between humans and things, but also the increased mobility of humans and of commodities during the period.

The narrative patterns of the It-narratives of the Enlightenment period were then propagated again in the avant-garde literature of the early twentieth century, reflecting an increased transnational mobility during this phase of intense global commerce and industrialization. For example, the Russian writer Sergei Tret'iakov formulated a literary program that he called *Biography of the Object* in 1929, which represented a polemical departure from the classic bourgeois novel. He recommends the following narrative pattern: "The compositional structure of the 'biography of the object' is a conveyor belt along which a unit of raw material is moved and transformed into a useful product through human effort" (Tret'iakov, 2006, p. 61).

Instead of revolving around individual heroes such as bourgeois personalities, Tret'iakov recommends writing about material things. Against the background of a materialistic worldview, by "things" Tret'iakov means especially substances: "Books such as *The Forest, Bread, Coal, Iron, Flax, Cotton, Paper,*

The Locomotive, and *The Factory* have not been written. We need them, and it is only through the 'biography of the object' that they can be adequately realized" (Tret'iakov, 2006, p. 62). Tret'iakov believed that "we can view class struggle synoptically at all stages of the production process" (Tret'iakov, 2006, pp. 61–62). The point here, then, as in the It-narratives, is to choose the mobile vantage point of an inanimate object in order to represent and critique problematic social relations. Materials mentioned by Tret'iakov, such as coal, iron, cotton, paper, and bread, lend themselves in a very special way as heroes of such stories because they have a very long and eventful life. With his literary concept, Tret'iakov brought to the fore a narrative style that enjoyed increasing popularity, especially among socialist storytellers. Tret'iakov himself referred to the novels of Pierre Hamp, who had treated seafood in a similar way in his socially critical novel series *La peine des hommes* (Hamp, 1936).

In fact, in the twentieth century this soon led to the development of nonfiction books that dealt exclusively with individual materials. These material histories can formally be seen as a fusion of It-narratives with paradoxical eulogies. Inanimate materials are indeed depicted in great detail, and usually praised for their extraordinary qualities. The methods highlighted by Fronto are also nearly always used (e.g. imagining the world without this or that substance). Equally, a "substance-in-motion" is usually depicted, which traverses different social environments. It is through the contrast of these environments that the tension and entertainment value of these "novels" arises.

The first direct predecessors of contemporary books on substances were published in the 1920s and 1930s. One of the first to have the courage to write a popular book about a single material was the writer and journalist Heinrich Eduard Jacob. He begins his book on coffee, published by Ernst Rowohlt in 1934, with an explanatory prologue:

> Not the vita of Napoleon or Caesar is told here,
> but the biography of a substance.
> Of a millennial, faithful and powerful companion of all mankind.
> A hero.
> As one might tell the biography of copper or wheat, so here is told
> the life of coffee among and with men. Its influence on the outer
> structure and the inner structure of society, its connection with its
> destinies and with the cause of those destinies. (Jacob, 1934)

This explanatory section was omitted from the English edition of the work, *Coffee*, that was published in 1998 (Jacob, 1998). This is understandable because the justification for an entire book on coffee no longer needed to be explained sixty-four years after the first publication of Jacob's influential book. Books of this type are nowadays well-known to the reader and do not deserve any excuses or explanations. Nevertheless, the introductory lines of the first edition are interesting because they make clear that at the time of the first edition the author had to explain himself, as something new had been undertaken in the work and it was necessary to briefly outline the literary concept guiding it. Jacob saw his coffee book as an innovative counterpart to the bourgeois novel. Its form was based on the biography, as he himself emphasized – not the biography of an important person, but the biography of a substance, a material. This material now travels like a mobile camera through very different countries and times.

At the same time, coffee is described, characterized, and praised in great detail. In fact, Jacob believes that substances, and especially coffee, are highly active. He credits coffee with an almost heroic drive. It interacts with human society, as he points out. It is not just passively used or shaped by society, but rather shapes society itself. He shows this by emphasizing the importance that coffee and the coffeehouse had as a pick-me-up during the Enlightenment period (Jacob, 1998, ch. 13). Coffee was linked to the cultural and political project of the Enlightenment thinkers, for just as the Enlightenment sought to enlighten people intellectually, so too coffee provided increased mental alertness.

Jacob's work, as can be seen in such passages, certainly has a claim to deliver knowledge; it aims to reveal cultural and economic connections that link different parts of the world via coffee. However, his primary intention is not to teach but to entertain, as becomes clear from correspondence with his publisher, Ernst Rowohlt. He does not regard his book on coffee as a contribution to science or popular education; the book is to him itself a commodity to be sold as much as possible (Soentgen, 2006). It assimilates itself into his object.

It can therefore be argued that the intention of this perhaps first modern novel on a substance is probably not very different from that of the paradoxical eulogies: Jacob, too, wants his books to captivate his readers, to entertain them. The goal of imparting knowledge is clearly subordinate to the goal of entertainment. What does not contribute to entertainment is shortened or omitted altogether. As a result, Jacob largely omits the negative and cruel aspects of the story of coffee in his material history and does not represent slavery on the coffee plantations or the ecological costs of coffee monocultures in any great detail.

As far as narrative technique is concerned, it can be noted that Jacob makes extensive use of the rhetorical devices recommended by the orator Fronto. There are numerous quotations from poets, a technique which already Fronto had recommended. In particular, Jacob makes abundant use of the method mentioned by Fronto of weaving "tales of gods" into the narrative. Indeed, coffee itself is represented by Jacob as being a divine being. At a central point in his biography, which deals with the spread of coffee in Europe, it says: "Beyond Nürnberg, there was no demand at all. For in Central Germany and North Germany coffee had to wrestle with a titan whose powers were enormously greater than those of Bacchus. This titan was the lord of Northern Europe. His name was Beer" (Jacob, 1998, p. 52). Here, the narrative pattern is of a fight of an Olympian against a titan.

Such adaptions of narrative patterns from ancient mythology are abundant in the book (Jacob, 1998, p. 139). Jacob expands the mythological storyline by having coffee compete not only against beer but also against tea. And here, too, his material extends into the superhuman, into the divine, because the decision between drinking coffee and tea is almost a religious one for him: "Throughout Europe, the Christo-Romanticists drank tea. This infusion influenced poetry, opinions, conversation. It promoted gentleness and thoughtfulness, but also emotionalism and sentimentality" (Jacob, 1998, p. 139). Thus, tea is virtually stylized as an anti-god who challenges coffee and, accordingly, the chapter on tea is titled "The Advance of Tea" (Jacob, 1998, p. 139).

Jacob's language is so permeated with rhetorical stylistic devices that it is noticeable when he does *not* make use of one. For example, he dispenses with the device of counterfactual fiction, which consists of imagining a world in which the touted material would not exist. Fronto, as I have pointed out, uses this at the very beginning of his speech on smoke and dust, and it is frequently found in the paradoxical eulogies. And not only there: in contemporary commercial advertising, this rhetorical figure is so ubiquitous that it is parodied (see, for example, the episode "Zinc Oxide and You" in *The Kentucky Fried Movie* [1977]). Jacob, however, does not need such a simple method because he lets the history of coffee unroll quite organically, namely, in such a way that each phase in the history of coffee arises from the previous one.

Jacob's biography of coffee – which he refers to as a novel – is much longer than the familiar paradoxical eulogies. To mitigate the problems this creates, it is divided into relatively short chapters. The chapters are never longer than twenty pages. Even though it cannot be assumed that Jacob was familiar with Fronto's recommendations on how to write paradoxical eulogies, it can be assumed that the classically educated Jacob knew the form of such eulogies. This is because classical writers who wrote these eulogies, for example Lucian, were part of the classical reading canon in grammar schools of the Habsburg monarchy. In any case, it is obvious that Jacob uses the rhetorical devices mentioned by Fronto frequently and as a central component of the work.

However, Jacob's novel, like most later material histories, cannot be understood simply as a somewhat lengthy paean to coffee. Contemporary material nonfiction, as already noted, has other sources as well. For Jacob, like the authors of the novels of circulation, uses his hero as a moving point of observation to explore contrasting social environments. The journey of coffee goes around the world, beginning in the "Land of Yemen," where the coffee bush grew wildly and was first cultivated, and ending in Brazil, which was then, as now, the main exporter of coffee. This reflects the increased circulation of goods and increased social mobility, as well as the increased interest in global contexts.

Numerous illustrations and caricatures, a total of eighteen text illustrations in the first edition as well as sixty illustrations in rotogravure, complement the work. Last but not least, *Coffee* utilizes a journalistic narrative style. For example, in the last pages of his work, Jacob tells the story of when he was on a flight in Brazil, near Santos, and witnessed the large-scale destruction of coffee beans carried out on the instructions of the state in order to stabilize the price of coffee (Jacob, 1998, pp. 260–265). This insertion of reportage not only provides an important piece of information but adds to the vividness of the account and thus to its entertainment value. The use of what was at the time the still extraordinary airplane, combined with the unusual perspective from above that it provided, make this passage exciting and authentic. The change of perspective and the adoption of a bird's-eye view were novel methods of narrating that were also inspired by the new medium of film that took hold of public imagination as motion pictures became a mass medium in Europe in the 1920s. The very fact that Jacob followed his material physically distinguishes his working method from that of many earlier authors. He thus aligns himself with his highly mobile substance. In 1932, in the course of his research for the book, Jacob had made a trip to Brazil. He had used a Zeppelin, boarding in Friedrichshafen on Lake Constance and disembarking in Recife in northeastern Brazil.

The use of journalistic methods of storytelling was easy for Jacob because he was a successful journalist, like many contemporary authors of material histories. He worked for the *Berliner Tageblatt*, whose Central European bureau in Vienna he had headed since 1927. His career as a writer and journalist ended abruptly when the National Socialists came to power in 1933, and he lost his position as head of the Vienna bureau. His work on coffee, *Sage und Siegeszug des Kaffees*, was, however, printed by Rowohlt in 1934, although distribution had to be taken over by a publisher in exile in Moravian Ostrava in order to circumvent the literary censorship practiced in the German "Reich." On March 22, 1938, eleven days after the so-called Anschluss of Austria, he was arrested as a Jew and opponent of National Socialism and deported to the Dachau concentration camp near Munich, from where he was later transferred to Buchenwald near Weimar. It was only thanks to the tireless efforts of his fiancée and later wife Dora Angel-Soyka that he was finally released and able to emigrate to the United States, where he again worked as a publicist, also publishing a history of another substance: *Six Thousand Years of Bread: Its Holy and Unholy History* (1944). After the end of the war he returned to Europe, but in spite of his former success as a writer and journalist he could not gain a foothold in postwar Germany. Jacob died in Salzburg in 1967.

Jacob is rightly considered by literary scholars to be one of the pioneers of modern nonfiction and especially of substance biographies (Clarenbach, 2002, pp. 123–131). *Coffee* is still being reprinted and read today. His book on bread is also still available in bookstores; it was required reading in schools in the United States (Clarenbach, 2002, p. 344). In Ulm in southern Germany, Heinrich Eduard Jacob's work even inspired a wealthy manufacturer of baked goods to found a bread museum in 1955.[1]

The extraordinary impact of Jacob's two biographies (Clarenbach, 2002, pp. 123–131) of substances underscores once again that he indeed succeeded in developing narrative methods that made it possible to write at book-length about a supposedly inanimate subject. If you now ask yourself how it is that these stories have achieved such popularity for around 100 years, it quickly becomes clear that several factors must be taken into consideration. Of course, this popularity is related to the fact that materials, as described in the first chapter, are becoming increasingly problematic for our societies. Some substances that are needed are in short supply, others are a nuisance or a danger because they suddenly appear in unexpected places, and still others are downright toxic. But these references to economic aspects, to health issues, and to the ecological problems of substances are likely to fall short, especially since these problems were barely in the public consciousness in the 1920s and 1930s when the first popular substance "novels" were written and found numerous readers.

Other factors are therefore likely to be relevant, and here it is worth recalling the thoughts of Lynn Festa (2015), who studied the popularity of It-narratives in the eighteenth century. For her, it was primarily social and cultural transformations that made it seem attractive to represent the world from the perspective of inanimate objects. The world, after all, became larger in eighteenth-century imperial Britain and, at the same time, it had also become more confusing and complex. Trade relations extended far beyond the British Isles. Goods circulated in increasing numbers and quantities, and society became more commodified. Things, especially

---

[1] Museum Brot und Kunst. https://museumbrotundkunst.de/en/museum.

goods, increasingly defined social relations; human labor became a commodity itself. Conversely, things themselves became increasingly social; indeed, they gained a certain personality. To entrust oneself to stories about substances, materials and goods in order to get to know society anew seemed obvious.

And so Lynn Festa writes: "At a moment in which the division of labor and the expansion of markets extended social and economic relations beyond the immediate purview of the individual, it-narratives suggest that things possess a perspective on society not available to the individuals or groups of which it is composed" (Festa, 2015, p. 340). Not only did the relationship between people, materials, and things change, but the relationships between people gained a new quality; the direct and indirect relations between actors, for example, became longer and more complex. Here, a kind of narrative that took the perspective of inanimate things, often commodities, promised a way to gain an overview. And, at the same time, things could reveal hidden secrets. As early as the eighteenth century, a silver spoon in a book for children and young adults could enlighten the adolescent reader about the connection between prosperity in the Western metropolis and misery in the mining regions of the colonial periphery (Festa, 2015, p. 346). The process of economic and cultural globalization and its tensions, to which the It-narratives of the eighteenth century repeatedly allude, continues into the present and is no longer confined to the society of the now defunct British Empire since nearly all countries have been affected by it.

This brief overview of the development of the genre of substance stories shows that these stories should not be considered in isolation; they are part of a larger family of narratives that revolve around unusual heroes. As shown in the eighteenth century by the It-narratives or novels of circulation, it need not be a substance that circulates. It can also be an insect or a thing, a coin, for example, or even a glass. But things are made of substances, and substances, compared to things, have much more complex and extended lives or "life cycles." This gives them a special status within the larger family of It-narratives. Only atoms have longer biographies, since they cannot be destroyed under normal circumstances and thus "live" forever, so to speak. Atom stories might be called the final literary consequence of substance stories. It is therefore no coincidence that one of the best-known collections of literary stories about substances, the justly much-praised work *Il sistema periodico* by the Italian chemist Primo Levi (1975, ch. "Carbonio"), ends with the story of a carbon atom because carbon "*dice tutto a tutti*" ("tells everything to everybody") (Levi, 1975, p. 230). Due to the importance of carbon in every biological process, carbon really has a lot to tell.

In order to place a material in the role of a story's protagonist, it is not only important that this very substance plays an important role in the economy of nature. There has to be something more. And this something more concerns its role in human society – in technology, economy, culture, and politics. If a certain substance is economically, politically, or culturally important, then there is a good chance that someone will write a story about it.

3 Research on the History of Individual Substances

What we have seen so far is that if we want to examine the narrative methods and intertextual references of contemporary material stories and histories, we do not necessarily need to take a closer look at any given substance itself. It is enough to analyze stories about substances, identifying the literary devices used in the text and its literary tradition, while considering the historical and cultural context of such stories. But is it really enough to restrict substance stories to a merely humanities based approach?

In any case, looking at the literary history of materials is not the only way of analyzing substances from a humanities perspective. There are also other approaches from a more environmental history perspective (see the contributions in Haumann et al., 2023) or from a science and technology studies perspective (see the contributions in Bensaude-Vincent et al., 2017). In these studies, the general history of It-narratives and of narratives on substances is not addressed. Here, the focus is not on the type of stories told about such substances in general, but about particular substances and their specific histories. From this perspective we can ask, for instance: What were the technical and infrastructural prerequisites that made the commodification of Helium possible (Zumbrägel, 2023)? How were certain novel substances like sex hormones framed in the public discourse in order to make commodification possible (Stoff, 2023)? How were fuel cells and hydrogen framed in twenty-first-century political discourse in Europe in order to make the transition from fossil energy to a "hydrogen world" possible (Teissier, 2017)? To answer such questions, an appropriate approach might be to begin by comparing circulating stories with each other and critically analyzing them with regard to the narrated contents. However, in doing so, it then becomes clear that one must also focus on the materials – the substances – themselves. Therefore, if we want to work on substances, we have to leave the comfort zone of the humanities. Whatever our specific perspective might be – whether we have a background in environmental history, science and technology studies, cultural studies, or something else – we must look not only at texts and their narratives, but also at specific substances and their behavior.

We will therefore have to specify what is meant by a substance. We will have to take a closer look at this or that specific substance. We will have to see it, touch it, smell it, and maybe even – if it is not toxic – taste it. We will have to learn something about its behavior. We do not have to become chemists or material scientists, but we should at least *try* to understand central aspects of chemical research on the substance at stake. It is not necessary to understand the latest developments of quantum mechanics in order to understand what a chemist says about "our" substance. But we should have the courage to at least talk with chemists and material scientists. We should have the courage to put on a white coat and safety goggles and enter a laboratory where research on "our" substance is being done. If we ignore this research, if we avoid directly encountering substances themselves, we will limit the range of our critical reflection. We will then only be able to work with second-hand knowledge.

Our aim should always be to try to reconstruct the history of a substance firsthand, that is, from primary sources. This does not only mean studying archival sources in their original language – something that any scholar of the humanities will agree is indispensable. It also means looking at the material and how it behaves. *The material is itself a primary source of knowledge.* Certainly, this way of doing research on the history of materials is a bit risky for scholars coming from the humanities because we will have to enter areas in which we are not trained. Research that not only includes materials from cultural archives but is also open to looking at specific substances and their behaviors will always have a slightly blurred disciplinary identity. It might not look the way a typical disciplinary contribution from the humanities is supposed to look. A certain amount of interdisciplinarity will be inevitable. However, it is precisely such work that is worthwhile and innovative, as I hope to show below in general, and then in particular, using the example of rubber.

Academic research on the history of substances has been around since about 1842. At that time, the French historian Ferdinand Hoefer published the first volume of his *Histoire de la Chimie*, which included over sixty sketches on the history of substances (Hoefer, 1866, second section). Somewhat later, the chemist and historian Hermann Kopp devoted the entire third and fourth volumes of his *History of Chemistry*, which is still indispensable today, to studies in the history of substances (Kopp, 1843–1847). James Riddick Partington, probably the most cited historian of chemistry in the twentieth century, took a biographical approach in his four-volume *History of Chemistry* (on Partington's method, see Weyer, 1974, pp. 192–200) and made individual chemists the starting point of his account. However, he also worked on the history of substances, especially black powder (Partington, 1960).

The historian of science Jost Weyer then comparatively elaborated on the special features of the substance-historical approach in his analysis of the chemical–historical method. He spoke of a special feature of the historiography of chemistry that distinguishes it from the other disciplines of the history of science, "since chemistry is concerned with the structure and transformation of substances" (Weyer, 1974, p. 6). Here, we see historians who are working on substance histories. They are in some sense typical scholars, using the methods of the humanities, browsing archives and comparing and interpreting older or newer documents, while at the same time they know about the substance in question from firsthand experience. Often, they have some type of scientific background or training or are at least open to crossing the border of the humanities in order to learn more about their topic.

So we see a combination of both firsthand knowledge of the substance itself and a methodology that is not a chemical one but follows the normal approach of historical research. However, these histories are generally often very narrow. Narratives of substances or substance novels, as discussed in Section 2, are not considered. Maybe the biography of this or that chemist comes into play, but apart from that the only narratives as such that count portray the chemical behavior of the substance. Thus the world of these histories mainly concerns the narrow space of the laboratory. These studies have, up until now, mostly been laboratory histories, focusing on experiments in the lab and their interpretation in journals, textbooks, and lectures. They are oriented around how certain substances behave in the laboratory and the different interpretations of them throughout history. Aspects that lead beyond the laboratory are considered only insofar as they concern their occurrence or their economic or technical features. Even in many recent studies on the history of substances, the focus continues to be on their theoretical interpretation, and thus again on aspects associated with the laboratory (see, for instance, Marty & Monin, 2003). Such laboratory histories of substances typically concern the way certain substances were (first) represented, to whom their discovery can be attributed, and how they were interpreted and for what reasons in different times and in different laboratories. Here, the scientific interpretation is the focus of the investigation: What motivated the scientific interpretation and what alternatives existed?

Such research on substance histories is indeed interdisciplinary; it takes into account the behavior of the substance, but it has its shortcomings. It privileges scientific knowledge and ignores other aspects. The focus is on scientific experiments and scientific interpretation, mostly inserted into a master-narrative of endless scientific and technological progress. But what we might call the "life of a substance" is not confined to the laboratory. Substances are not only objects of research. They are bought and sold, produced, used and consumed, feared and praised, banned and disposed of. They do not only display scientifically predictable behavior according to scientific theories; they also lead a life of their own. They resurface in unexpected places and force us to deal with them again and again.

A somewhat different approach to the history of materials seems appropriate. It should focus on the life of substances in a broader way (Huppenbauer & Reller, 1996). In this sense, it is possible to look at the life of substances *beyond* the laboratories and *beyond* the plants that produce them.

By following the path of substances (Appadurai, 1986) beyond the laboratory door, ecological and political contexts, and ecological and social side effects and their narrative representations, come into view. We encounter not only scientific interpretations that might be rationally reconstructable but also semi-scientific opinions and stories that are completely fictional but which nevertheless circulate. As these nonscientific stories also influence the social handling of substances, they merit some attention.

Recent histories of substances, such as those on heroin (de Ridder, 2000), DDT (Simon, 1999, pp. 105–192), CFCs (Böschen, 2000, ch. 3), Agent Orange (Martini, 2012, see also Feinberg, 2012, pp. 23–40), napalm (Neer, 2013), chlorine (Chang & Jackson, 2007), plastics (Meikle, 1995 and also Westermann, 2007), aluminum (Marschall, 2008), and synthetic sex hormones (Marks, 2001), almost always include such stories. They not only focus on the controlled and rational space of the laboratory, but also look beyond this clear but also sometimes misleading space. In the laboratory we see rational intentions and interpretations. It is a space that is often interpreted as one of control and rationality. However, substances are not confined to this climatized and sterilized space. Once a given substance has become a commodity it leaves this space and more generally becomes an object of exchange. We must then accompany it. If we leave the laboratory, we will encounter unknown and unintended, and often unimagined, side effects and aftereffects of certain substances. As such phenomena exist and belong to the history of this or that substance, it is not recommended to limit the field of observation to the laboratory, the lecture hall, or scientific journals. We should also follow the substance as it moves out beyond the laboratory and factory doors.

Such a broadening of the field of observation, which is characteristic of recent research in the history of materials, not only brings scientific knowledge into view; it also leads into the important realm of nonscientific knowledge. Nonscientific knowledge is not only important in a very general, philosophical sense for the history of certain substances; it can also set the history of certain substances in motion.

I will try to show in the following that the expansion of the field of observation, as practiced by recent research on the history of materials, brings actors and forms of knowledge into view that have so far received little or only stereotypical attention (Schilling & Vogel, 2019 and Pretel & Camprubí, 2018). At the same time, this research into the history of materials is creating a more accurate and very exciting picture of our contemporary material culture. A purely scientific view of substances and materials is not exhaustive and complete; rather, it obscures important aspects. Even life-cycle assessments, which in their own way attempt to examine substances beyond the factory gates and look at the side effects of their use, are necessarily limited because they have to focus on quantifiable aspects. However, substance history studies are about understanding interrelationships. From a more accurate and comprehensive understanding of the way contemporary material culture has evolved, it will be possible to more realistically assess how our material culture could be transformed toward greater sustainability.

Before taking a specific example – the history of rubber – to demonstrate why research into the history of substances is rewarding, I would like to briefly explain what I understand by the basic concepts of substance and history.

4 Substances and Materials

Throughout the Element, I use the terms "substance," "matter," "material," and even "stuff" interchangeably as if they had more or less the same meaning. Of course, a substance is not exactly the same as a material or stuff. However, what is meant is a certain type of material object. Examples of such objects are sand, water, sugar, paper, dirt, cocaine, cotton, and so on. Now I will try to explain what I mean by the concept of a substance or material.

From basic chemistry, we know that substances are divided into mixtures and pure substances and the pure substances into elements and compounds. All in all, the natural sciences say that all substances are forms of matter. On this view, matter is everything that occupies space and has a defined mass, with space and mass described in more detail in theoretical physics. Following this trail, one will very quickly leave behind the common everyday experience in which one handles substances and find oneself in a discourse on elementary particles that cannot be understood without knowledge of higher mathematics.

However, the concept of a substance does not automatically have to be connected with a scientific concept. There are other starting points. People have been talking about stuff or materials long before the beginning of modern science. The concept of a substance can therefore be grounded in everyday experience. Indeed, the concept of a substance is a fundamental concept of everyday life. This means that everybody deals with substances whether they understand anything about modern chemistry or not. We all cook, eat, and drink, and in doing so necessarily handle substances and have a basic understanding of them. Even the most complicated activity of the chemist in the laboratory is termed in laboratory slang as "cooking," and indeed we find the same basic activities – namely, weighing, measuring, mixing, dissolving, heating, and so on – as in the kitchen. Even the equipment, from a functional point of view, is not as different as it might at first seem.

It is therefore possible to develop a phenomenological concept of a substance (Soentgen, 2008). I will try to clarify the meaning of this concept by going back to everyday experiences that are as easily accessible as possible (instead of the latest scientific theories). In this way, a preliminary understanding can be developed that serves as a guide for further research. It is true that no culture-independent "essence of things" can be achieved by a phenomenological methodology. However, the value of the phenomenological method is that it is much more independent of specialized contexts of experience and therefore less dependent on theoretical presuppositions than, say, modern scientific knowledge. It offers a comparatively low-level entry point with few prerequisites and therefore a stable starting point for further research, which is also helpful for transcultural questions.

For these reasons, unrefined everyday experience has not only been recommended by phenomenology. In American pragmatism, too, John Dewey in particular presented a much-noted defense of experience, and here primarily of ordinary, nonspecialized experience (see Dewey, 1925, ch. 1). He writes: "We may begin with experience in gross, experience in its primary and crude forms, and by means of its distinguishing features and its distinctive trends, note something of the constitution of the world which generates and maintains it" (Dewey, 1925, p. 5). That does not mean that the more refined forms of scientific experience are negligible. Much to the contrary, we should try to integrate them: "Those who start with coarse, everyday experience must bear in mind the findings of the most competent knowledge" (Dewey, 1925, p. 5).

Phenomenology is about working out the core of certain phenomena (Zahavi, 2019, pp. 86–100). The aim of phenomenological descriptions is to provide as rich an account as possible of the phenomenon itself. Questions that help in fulfilling such an analysis are: How do we get acquainted with a certain phenomenon? What are typical examples of the phenomenon Are there similar phenomena that might allow us to make comparisons? If we compare one type or class of phenomena with another, it is often easier to see typical features.

And in the end, as Dewey says, it is important to "bear in mind the findings of the most competent knowledge." That is to say, it makes sense to establish links between the findings of a phenomenological analysis of everyday experience and chemistry and physics.

The important thing about phenomenology is not to neglect science, but to set up the inquiry from a different starting point. This makes sense because scientific experience is not only "more competent," as Dewey says, but often very specialized. Only measurable data is appreciated, with qualitative aspects often slipping through the net of the scientist. The resulting knowledge is certainly competent, but it is at the same time often too abstract and narrow.

In this Element, substances are therefore not understood as mere scientific objects, but rather as everyday phenomena (Soentgen, 1997, also 2019, pp. 18–23). We deal with substances on a daily, even hourly basis. We write on paper. We refill the printer toner. Or, even more basic, we wash the dirt off carrots, we drink milk, salt pasta, and so on. Hunger and thirst are generally an important and probably the original reason why we distinguished substances from other phenomena.

Regardless of language and cultural background, all people depend on drinking clean, fresh water. Our oral senses are attuned to substances. Sugar and salt, for example, which look very similar, can be easily distinguished by tasting them. We also recognize sour milk more easily by smell or taste than by mere visual appearance (Mizrahi 2014). Our oral sense, which combines tasting and smelling, also warns us of toxic substances. Bitter foods, for example, while appreciated in some contexts, initially evoke defensiveness and disgust in children, and not without reason. Very many toxic substances have a bitter taste.

It is true that different cultures think very differently about substances. In the history of European science, we find many different ways of analyzing the world of substances. On the other hand, certain kinds of substances are classified similarly in different parts of the world, and this is to be expected in view of the fact that the human body has similar needs the world over, with some substances providing food or drink and others being hazardous poisons. All around the world people know of certain kinds of substances such as salt, flour, honey, and so on. Aside from these, there are substances that are used nearly everywhere around the world to produce certain things like clay, wood, or sand. Substances that have a strong physiological effect are also known to almost all cultures, especially alcoholic beverages.

Now, our contemporary world is characterized by the fact that it has brought into circulation a previously unknown variety of substances that are not found in nature and which were unknown in earlier times, such as nylon, perlon, polyethylene terephthalate (PET), PVC, and aluminum, to name just a few. These synthetic substances are substances nonetheless, just like salt or sand, even though they originated in a laboratory.

A substance is therefore a material entity that differs in a specific way from other material entities. Materiality is a property that characterizes substances, things, and living beings. There are also immaterial objects, such as rays of light, for example. Phenomenologically, it can be demonstrated that the sensory complexity of material objects, compared to immaterial objects, is significantly higher. You do not only see substances, you can usually also elicit sounds or even tones from them, you can smell or taste them, you can touch them, you can also feel gases and liquids on the skin. You can usually also store them, which is only indirectly possible with immaterial objects.

To further clarify the general meaning of "substance," it helps to work with a contrast. It makes sense to distinguish substances (such as sugar or chocolate) from things (such as chairs or books). Both are material objects. However, they are distinctively different. Substances differ from things in that they can be portioned, that is, divided in any direction without losing their identity. For example, if you divide a piece of chocolate into two portions, the result is still chocolate. However, if you tear a thing in half, for example a book, you do not get two books but rather "a torn book" or "a torn piece of paper." Substances are most often referred to in connection with some indication of quantity, as for example when one says "some salt" or "a pinch of salt." When it comes to things, however, there is an expectation that they are complete, so to speak, as for example when one talks about "the fork" or "the knife" or, alternatively, "a knife" or "a fork." With substances, we are always dealing with a certain portion, a sample.

This feature of portionability constitutes the better-known part of the concept of a substance. However, as we know from ordinary everyday experience, there is another important part of the concept: substances always develop their own activity. They distribute themselves throughout the world, mix, and transform themselves. For example, once released from its packet, flour distributes itself, immediately filling in little cracks as it spreads across a table, and it does not voluntarily return to its packet. If it is mixed with another powder, say sugar, the mix cannot be completely separated. This tendency is so ubiquitous it is easy to overlook it. Other tendencies are more specific to certain substances. Iron rusts, copper soon becomes covered in copper rust, silver develops a black topping, and even gold, which is a symbol of immutability, changes over time. A green-brown film known as patina can develop on gold coins, for example.

Substances therefore not only have *aptitudes* or suitabilities by which they can be completely integrated into human activities (except, perhaps, for an overlooked residue), they also have tendencies. They have an autonomous activity which can be slowed down for a while, but which can never be completely switched off, nor can it be predicted with certainty in advance. This autonomous activity is specific to each substance, with a given substance identifiable by its tendencies. Of course, such tendencies depend on the environment the substance is in, yet the tendency originates from the substance itself. This aspect is, as previously mentioned, demonstrable from a purely phenomenological point of view, although it can, of course, also be explained with scientific concepts, in particular the concept of so-called chemical potential, a quantitative conceptualization of thermodynamics.

The tendencies of substances lead to their stubborn behavior, which manifests itself in space and time. On the one hand, we find autonomous dispersal and migration movements of certain substances and, on the other hand, specific transformation tendencies: substances transform, crystallize, condense, evaporate, become brittle or bleach, or combine with other substances, and so on. The behavior of certain substances in certain material environments can only be studied very selectively in the laboratory. The transformation of substances and thus also their ecological or physiological effects can therefore only be predicted to a fairly limited extent. There are also limits to computer simulation, which is mainly useful when the processes and the framework conditions of a given environment are well-known, such as with the simulation of defined production processes within industrial plants. But what happens if something goes wrong, as when substances are released out into the open? Their behavior and effects cannot be predicted with the same accuracy. Consequently, any substance is only partially controllable.

One special tendency is found in every substance: a portion of any given substance, be it a liquid, a gas, or a solid, will try to dissipate, to spread out into the world. This tendency is best known in liquids and gases, but it is also pertinent to solids. The ancient Greeks observed that even solid rings made out of very hard and noble substances, like gold, get thinner as time goes by. They lose particles.

This specific and at the same time general tendency is not only of theoretical interest. It is significant for the history of substances given that as soon as substances are released into the open they start to autonomously move and transform, and in doing so they cross boundaries: the boundaries of bodies and ecosystems, as well as political boundaries. They start stories in which they are not only passive objects but also actors. The activity of substances implies that not only do people do things with substances but substances also do things with people.

In this context, the concept of activity must be used with caution, as it has perhaps become all too fashionable. In some instances, talk of self-activity might be more of a rhetorical device than the hallmark of an innovative phenomenological description. For example, if we read that "plastic is conquering the world," we should be cautious. Often such metaphors have the goal of obscuring the actual processes by assigning to the substance an activity or making a certain phenomenon look like an inevitable fate when it is actually the result of activities of quite specific industrial actors. In the same way, we might question whether the sentence "heroin enslaves your soul" has any clear meaning. For the strong effects that heroin or other substances have on the body and mind is by no means to be sought in what might be called its malignant or even diabolical character. Such attributions are socially constructed and obscure rather than illuminate the underlying facts. Therefore, the very popular concept of self-activity, or so-called agency, is always to be used with caution. Although it is undeniable that substances do develop activity, our efforts should be based on describing this activity as accurately as possible, always considering whether alternative descriptions are available.

As soon as substances leave the laboratory, they begin to mix. You can isolate them, but of course these isolated objects are only an elaborately manufactured artificial product that is not "naturally there" (Ruthenberg, 2022, ch. 3). Wherever pure substances are shown or sold to us, be it iron, PVC, gold, silver, platinum, copper, salt, "pure cotton," "pure silk," or even medical preparations, we can be sure that next to every crumb or drop of pure substance, a bucket of air exhaust, sewage, waste, or debris could be placed beside it that was unintentionally but inevitably coproduced during its production (Schlaudt, 2021). Indeed, everyday experience teaches us that completely pure, isolated substances hardly ever occur: even clear water contains dissolved limestone and air, as can be seen immediately when it is heated. Where there are substances, they have the tendency to mix with each other, to combine. Substances are sociable beings, always ready to mix and spread.

Based on such phenomenological considerations, substances and things can be clearly distinguished conceptually. However, substances and things also remain closely connected. Things are made of substances. Almost every thing that we deal with in everyday life is a sample of a substance or of several combined substances. Where this is not the case, as for example with a rainbow or a hologram, it is an immaterial phenomenon.

As things very often "consist" of this or that substance, things usually provide a good opportunity to learn something about a given substance. This was pointed out by early phenomenologists, with Heidegger coining the concept of *Zuhandenheit* (ready-to-hand) (Heidegger, 1927, p. 69) which, according to him, shapes our everyday dealings with things and indicates our intuitive knowledge of their usability. We know what this or that thing is suitable for. This suitability is twofold as it refers to the purpose and to the substance, and one *sees* the suitability of the substance of which the thing is made. Therefore, by observing things and their use one usually also learns something about the substances of which the things are made. This seemingly trivial observation is of interest for material histories because it allows us to build a bridge between more ethnological research on material culture and research on the history of science and technology. In the case of rubber, someone unfamiliar with this material would still be able to see from its use in children's toys what it is suitable for. One might infer, or even assume, from observing a child playing with a rubber alligator, for example, that the material is nontoxic, that it is elastic and not sharp-edged, that it is likely to be durable enough to withstand the child's play, that it floats on water, that it can be molded into any shape, and so on. If someone sees a bouncing rubber ball, they also learn something about rubber, even if for the time being that substance is unknown to them.

The fact that information about unknown substances can be derived from things that are made out of them is not only essential to the history of rubber but also to other substance stories – for example, the history of phosphorus. Here, the mere observation by a chemist of the fascinating substance produced by an alchemist named Henning Brand was almost sufficient for that observer to produce the phosphorus himself and subsequently to claim invention of the substance (Roth, 2021, see also Soentgen, 2021). The very experienced alchemist Johannes Kunckel, who visited Brand, could see that it was a novel material with a waxy consistency that shed a pale light in the dark. Kunckel could smell that urine was an important part of the production process of phosphorus, and it was not difficult to see that distillation was the central operation. From here, only a little additional information was needed to determine the process that actually produced phosphorous.

5 Histories and Stories

Doing research on the history or stories of this or that substance results in novel stories and histories. These will often have an interdisciplinary touch as they try to take into account not only concepts from the humanities but also the results of scientific work on the substance. This might be seen as an effort to overcome the disadvantages of the scientific division of labor (Ertl & Soentgen, 2015, see also Soentgen & Reller, 2009 and Emeis & Schlögl-Flierl, 2021). Ideally, the result is not a colorful juxtaposition of disparate information but rather a coherent history.

But what is meant by stories in the plural? How do stories differ from other forms of representation, especially from theories?

A *story* is a narrative representation of actions (Ricoeur, 1984 and Köller, 2006). It is divided into phases that follow one another and are interrelated, such as beginning, middle, and end. Stories can be fact-based or fictional. Fact-based stories that refer to events of the past are called histories. Stories are probably the oldest medium for the representation and communication of knowledge; they often also have a legitimizing function (Cronon, 1992, also Pankau, 1994). If one compares them with conceptual, theory-based forms of representation, stories are less accurate but have more integrative power. This means they involve the listener and/or reader more, especially at an emotional level. They address the whole person and not just the intellect. *Histories* are nothing but a special subtype of stories. They are more reflexive, methodologically elaborated, and pretend at least to be thoroughly fact-based. Their aim is to represent facts of the past; in contrast, a story can also include fictional materials. There can be stories about totally fictional matters like unobtainium; however, there cannot be a true history of unobtainium. Instead one might write a history about stories of unobtainium (Bartolovich 2017).

In terms of the analytical aspect of research into the history of substances, the concept of action is central. It refers to actions such as interpreting, prospecting, transforming, producing, exchanging or selling, using and consuming, regulating by law, burning, burying and dumping substances. It can refer to individual actions or to collective actions, that is, actions individuals perform with others (Janich, 2001, p. 44f.). A detailed analysis of the actions (and omissions) of individual or collective actors involved in the production, trade, use, and disposal of materials shows that "material flows," which in many representations are almost naturalized, usually run from south to north (Espahangizi, 2014, p. 204) and are always composed of chains of actions that are therefore socially mediated.

Actions are therefore the focus of material histories. Such actions can take place in very concrete social and cultural contexts, in specific historical situations, and can be those of either individual or collective actors, who act on the basis of identifiable motives. Often, these actions can only be accurately evaluated with sufficient historical distance.

The materials themselves are by no means neutral masses, as they appear in the very influential cultural studies of Arjun Appadurai (Soentgen, 2019, pp. 39–44), for example. They have, as new materialism has rightly emphasized, their very own life. It is always worthwhile, before turning to sources and documents, to gain as comprehensive an impression as possible of the material itself, to get to know its behavior, its smell, how it feels, to engage intensively with it. Here, too, the phenomenological method can be valuable. Indeed, it offers the possibility of clarifying general ontological concepts – such as those of substance or thing – by taking into account everyday experiences. It also makes it possible to gain a rich and complex *impression* of very specific substances, which can then also fertilize the following analyses, as I will show using the example of rubber.

Material histories start with this or that material and then try to study it in order to become more knowledgeable about it. Research into substance history asks a series of questions: How did the substance come into the world? Where did it come from? How has it transformed? How was it interpreted? What stories have been told about it and with which impact? Substance histories, unlike life-cycle assessments, do not deal with material flows; rather, they try to avoid naturalizing their subject. After all, they are not concerned with purely natural phenomena, such as the flow of lava during a volcanic eruption. The stories of substances are socially and culturally mediated. Their subjects are vast, historically evolved cooperative relationships, networks of agents, unintended third parties, and involve ecosystems and materials. This is further complicated by the fact that every purposeful action has side effects, some of which are desired or tolerated, but many of which turn out to be unforeseen and undesired. The activity of substances also contributes to the known unknowns and the unknown unknowns of what will happen with the substance. Such activities may be expected from the outset, but they can also *happen to* the actors or, even more frequently, to unintended third parties.

For example, CFCs diffuse into the atmosphere and have unforeseen effects in the stratosphere, which in turn trigger human activities. This interaction of material activity and human actions and interpretations of them is a decisive part of the dramaturgy of many material stories.

Research into the history of substances finds not only networks of actions and moving substances but also discovers already circulating stories. These are stories of the origin of certain substances, of their powers, of the people who have or had (or will have) to deal with them. These stories are an important part of the life of substances; they deserve to be collected and reflected upon. It often turns out, for example, that they have certain recurring structural principles (so called 'plots') that make them easily circulable, but that they are also often problematic in terms of their content. Collecting and analyzing such patterns is an important part of research into the history of materials (for narratives on the first discovery of quinine, see Gänger, 2021, pp. 30–53). In the end, the goal is to tell a polyphonic and reflective story about the history of a given material. Thus, as everywhere in the humanities, the result of the research becomes part of the area of research. There is a certain circle or a spiral: we start with stories and end with stories.

Stories are usually structured and organized by what can be called a narrative schema or narrative form. In many cases, we also speak of a plot. The plot is an integrative element that gives stories coherence and prevents the narrative from falling apart into a series of events, into a mere chronicle. It is a very important sort of cognitive organizer. We know plots primarily from literature, from novels or films. The British novelist E. M. Forster has given a coherent definition of the plot in his *Aspects of the Novel*. He writes:

> We have defined a story as a narrative of events arranged in their time-sequence. A plot is also a narrative of events, the emphasis falling on causality. "The king died and then the queen died" is a story. "The king died, and then the queen died of grief" is a plot. The time-sequence is preserved, but the sense of causality overshadows it. (Forster, 1969, p. 82)

Research has demonstrated that such plots are present also in contemporary historical studies. The French historian Paul Veyne even places them at the center of historical work. He writes:

> Facts do not exist in isolation, in the sense that the substance of history is what we shall call a plot, a very human and not very "scientific" mixture of material causes, aims, and chances – a slice of life, in short, that the historian cuts as he wills and in which facts have their objective connections and their relative importance. (Veyne, 1984, p. 32)

Veyne emphasizes that there is never just one plot that organizes a given material: "Historians relate plots, which are like so many itineraries that they mark out at will through the very objective field of events ... no historian describes the whole of this field, for an itinerary cannot take every road; none of these itineraries is the true one, is History" (Veyne, 1984, p. 36). This does not mean that there could not be better and less good roads. Rather, it means, first and foremost, that it is important to develop a special sensitivity toward and awareness of typical plots in order to then have the courage to explore new paths. Veyne's doctrine of plot as the basic narrative structure of scholarly history has received much approval. Paul Ricoeur (1984, pp. 288–338) has adopted and expanded on it. A critical sensitivity to such plots is essential for research into the history of materials. In the narratives devoted to substances typical of modernity, we often find very typical plots.

This brings me back to the "king" who played the main role in Forster's definition of the plot. A certain familiarity with material-historical literature quickly shows that it is not only people but also certain materials that are called "kings." There are narratives not only about King Edward VIII, but also novels about "King Coal" and "King Cotton." Even such a hyperbolic designation of this or that substance as a 'king' implies a plot. One must then tell how it came to "rule" this or that substance and against which previous "ruler" the substance prevailed. Furthermore, it is usually implied that certain substances are not only used locally but worldwide. They then establish a "world empire." Often Europeans play a decisive role in this, be it as discoverers, scientists, or as economic profiteers.

The plot of the king and his empire can be further refined by reporting in more detail on how the reign was shaped, for example as a "reign of terror" or as a period characterized by more or less general prosperity. One can then deepen the narrative by describing who benefited most from this rule and who may have been left behind. Finally, this type of plot can also tell of the end of the reign, of how a particular king lost his rule. The plainness of the plot of the king in no way hinders its popularity, even in contemporary times. Where it is told rather ironically, or seemingly quoted only from a great distance, it still structures the account and acts as a "cognitive organizer."

This popular plot can be criticized from the point of view of research into the history of materials. It is obvious that this kind of narration tends to naturalize events – paradoxically, by declaring a certain substance to be the "king," that is, by personifying it. Supernatural powers are attributed to a certain material by virtue of which it rules. In the process, it easily happens that the actual actors are made invisible, and the fact that the story could have taken a completely different course is obscured. But also if actors are actually named, some critical questions should be asked: Did they really have the role that is ascribed to them? It is typical of the plots of many popular histories of materials, as they were told up to the 1990s and in many cases still today, that the thematized material was attributed in one way or another to the work of European or US-American scientists – be it that it came into the world through their work, that they decisively improved it, that they gave it a new name, or that as consequence of their work the substance could be produced in a more efficient way: Only European or US-American entrepreneurs and researchers bring this or that substance to its "throne," not infrequently "in one fell swoop." In the process, the contribution of earlier generations or the contribution of people in other parts of the world is often reduced or omitted altogether. It is therefore necessary to critically question the way in which a particular plot structures and organizes the attribution of performance and ingenuity.

A second critical aspect is the way in which the actual materiality of a material is perspectivized by the plot. Where a certain material is personified and called "king," for example, it is also often spiritualized. Similarly, since the Middle Ages two bodies have been attributed to the king (Kantorowicz, 1957), a natural-material body and a political body, and there is a similar trend today to reduce a substance to its social-economic functions, omitting its other, material body.

The substance is identified with its social functions, its effects, and the economic organizations, legal institutions, and political structures that attach to it, that is, to its social effects. After their "reign," these "kings" leave behind practically no material traces and, if they do, it is only those that can be found in archives. They seem to simply melt into the air at the end of their reign.

However, this contradicts modern insights into the structure and nature of matter as well as our simple everyday experiences. This is because in reality substances are transformed by use – they crumble with time, decay into dust, seep away, and evaporate without actually disappearing. They become scrap, waste, broken pieces of rubbish, dust, or even noxious gases, thus remaining part of the environment. In many cases, it is only then that they develop a true life of their own; their actual material life, so to speak, is only just beginning. It is therefore important to include these phases in stories that really seek to investigate the life of a given material.

What, for example, remains of "King Rubber," the rubber that has been transformed into microrubber, fine dust, or old tire dumps in deserts (Tamis et al., 2021), which are so huge they can be seen from space. It is necessary to look not only at the social functions of such "kings," but also to make their materiality the subject of discussion. We probably have to say farewell to narratives that revolve around "kings," though, because this metaphor pushes the people involved with such materials too far into the background. This means that new plots are needed for stories about materials. These new plots may not sound as catchy as the old ones, but they will make us aware of new and different aspects, paving the way for new insights into the past and new ideas for the future.

In summary, material histories deal with specific concrete materials which are (1) described phenomenologically and (2) then examined within a historically evolved context of action that describes how materials were and are set on their way and released into the environment in an intended or unintended manner. In doing so, such material histories consider (3) the intrinsic activity of substances, which is part of their context of action and includes what sustains them and what often also thwarts them, as well as what remains after all purposeful action has ended, thus giving rise to new action. Such histories (4) collect stories that are already circulating about such materials and then analyze them to finally tell (5) a new, revised, polyphonic story. This definition is very general in order to capture the majority of actual research in the history of substances that can actually be encountered in the humanities, especially in the environmental humanities. It says nothing about a specific methodology like, for example, discourse analysis or ethnographic methods. This does not mean that I think that such methods are unimportant; however, it is inappropriate to include them in this definition that only aims to give an initial orientation.

The example of rubber will be used to illustrate that material histories enable a real deepening of our understanding of substances. At the same time, such a method has an integrative effect given that it elaborates inter-actions between scientific and nonscientific knowledge and connects the history of science and technology with overarching themes, thus bringing the research of substances out of the isolation in which it is often conducted. In this way, material histories contribute to a new understanding of our material world and our material culture.

6 The Origins of Rubber

Almost everyone today knows rubber. It is a peculiar, fascinating material, which many people become familiar with as children since many things made for them, especially for young children, are made of rubber (or novel elastomers that replace rubber). Teats and pacifiers and all kinds of balls, balloons, and other toys are made of rubber. Rubber is recommended as a material for use in things that small children come into contact with because it is light, and can be stretched in any direction without losing its original form. Rubber feels warm and has something skin-like about it; it can feel strangely alive, even though it is a dead material. It even has something like a voice; it can squeak and whisper, almost like living beings. It is no surprise, then, that objects that are intended to encourage play are often made of rubber, such as the so-called squeaking duck, a floating rubber duck.

Rubber products are rather good-natured in that they are not easily destroyed even in the hands of children. You can even bite into them. They are durable, as few other materials are, making them difficult to destroy. Products made of rubber are neither easily torn nor smashed. They are resistant and tough like leather, but unlike leather they can take on any shape. In a peculiar way, they combine flexibility – rubber products can be stretched and bent in any direction – with inflexibility. No matter what is done to them, products made of rubber always return to their original shape. They seem to have a certain memory.

Today, rubber is a rather imprecise term, as there are many different sub-stances that are referred to as rubber. Originally (and until the beginning of the twentieth century), most rubber originated from the so-called rubber tree (*Hevea brasiliensis*), as well as a few other tree species. Today, *Hevea brasiliensis* is still used for extracting latex from which rubber is produced. High performance products like condoms and airplane tires are still made of natural rubber, which has some advantages over synthetic rubber. However, a lot of rubber products today are made of synthetic rubber. Additives and a variety of different production processes are used to produce defined rubber qualities – for example, rubbers that are very soft or very hard. Despite this variety, the bulk of modern rubber products still share the same basic molecular structure and the same properties. The most important characteristic of rubber is its extraordinary elasticity. Elasticity is a form of stability. Solid rubber balls not only bounce higher and further and more often than other balls, they can also change direction easily – seemingly of their own volition. This feature, along with durability, is probably rubber's most impressive aspect.

The first stories that were told in Europe about rubber were forms of hyperbolic praise for an extraordinary substance that exemplified the "wonders of the New World." Rubber was used by Indigenous peoples in many places in South and Central America. The Jesuit Bernabé Cobo, who spent sixty-one years in South and Central America, wrote that it was *"bien conocido en todas las Indias"* ("well-known throughout the Americas") (Cobo, 1964, p. LXXIX (1), p. 268). The Spanish conquistador Gonzalo Fernández de Oviedo, who had personally met Christopher Columbus in his youth, spoke of the rubber balls of the Indians as if they were a miracle: "These balls bounce incomparably, because when they are thrown on the ground once with the hand, they bounce up again much higher and do another bounce and another and another and many [more]" (Fernández de Oviedo, 1992/1535, p. 145).[2] Bartolomé de Las Casas, who also describes rubber balls and the games associated with them in detail, even claims that the balls bounced for nearly a quarter of an hour (*"casi un cuarto de hora de saltar no cesa"*) (Las Casas, 1971, p. 23). As Las Casas reports, Christopher Columbus brought such a ball, which was reportedly as big as a jug (*"grande como una botija"*), from the New World to Seville (Las Casas, 1971, p. 23). These balls seemed almost alive and charged with energy. There was nothing like it in Europe. Rubber was in the material world what the sensitive mimosa was in the field of plants, an astonishing paradox. Just as the mimosa almost behaved like an animal, rubber seemed to be almost alive.

It was not only children who were fascinated by the strange lively elasticity of rubber. From the beginning, it has stimulated the imagination in Europe, with rubber long considered an almost miraculous material. Even more than 200

---

[2] Translated from Spanish: "Estas pelotas saltan . . . sin comparación, porque de solo soltalla de la mano en tierra, suben mucho más para arriba, e dan un salto, e otro e otro, y muchos."

years later, rubber had lost nothing of its fascination. In 1743, the French naturalist Pierre Barrère wrote euphorically about rings made of rubber:

> "The rings are even more admirable. . . . A ring, for example, which exactly encloses the five fingers of the hand when they are pressed together, can be stretched so as to let through not only an arm, but even the whole body. It then contracts again and, by its own elasticity, returns to its former state" (Barrère, 1743, p. 141).[3]

The novel properties of rubber made it appear almost animate, as the chemist and rubber researcher Friedrich Wilhelm Lüdersdorff emphasized a few decades later, writing: "Its extraordinary . . . elasticity ranks it, as it were, with living organisms" (Lüdersdorff, 1832, p. 15). Again, a few years later, the American rubber pioneer Charles Goodyear even sensed the wisdom of God in rubber: "There is probably no other inert substance, the properties of which excite in the human mind, when first called to examine it, an equal amount of curiosity, surprise, and admiration. Who can examine, and reflect upon this property of gum-elastic, without adoring the wisdom of the Creator?" (Goodyear, 1939, p. 23).

Rubber products display a certain cheerfulness through their surprising mobility, their tittering and flittering and their bouncing and jumping, so much so that they persuade you to play with them. Because rubber has no sharp edges, you can't cut yourself on it, unlike products made of wood, glass, or metal. Even more than foam, rubber is a typically fun material that virtually invites you to play with its mostly harmless stubbornness. The difficult to describe mixture of the mechanical and the quasi-living creates a comical impression. Rubber can wriggle and wiggle like a clown, an impression well captured by Gottfried Semper, who in 1860 devoted a separate section to rubber (or *caoutchouc*) in the first volume of his widely read work *Der Stil in den technischen und tektonischen Künsten oder Praktische Ästhetik (Style in the Technical and Tectonic Arts or Practical Aesthetics)*. He referred to rubber as an "ape among materials" (Semper, 1878, pp. 105–112, see p. 105). Whenever strange and unknown worlds full of wonders were imagined, as in the early 1913 science fiction novel *Lesabéndio* by Paul Scheerbart, rubber or rubber-like materials were part of the scenery (Scheerbart, 2012).

In the twentieth century, rubber appeared in entertainment genres of popular culture and still an atmosphere of extraordinarity surrounded it. For example, in

---

[3] Translated from French: "Les Anneaux sont encore bien plus admirables. . . . Un Anneau, par exemple, qui serre exactement les cinq doigts de la main, réunis ensemble, peut s'etendre assez pour laisser passer, non-seulement le bras, mais encore tout le corps: il se rétrecit ensuite, & devient, par sa propre élasticité, dans son premier état."

the 1961 Disney film *The Absent-Minded Professor*, the hero invents a material called "flubber," whose elasticity is increased to such an extent that on impact it recoils not only with almost the same amount of energy but with more. In the film, it was therefore also used to produce shoe soles, which made it possible – and, as it turns out, not only possible but inevitable – for humans to jump higher and higher with a single leap. Flubber is a word composed of "flying" and "rubber." In the German version of the film, it was called "Flummi" (from "Fliegen" and "Gummi"), a word that has survived in everyday German to this day and means small rubber balls. In the 1960s, the comic-strip character "Elongated Man" was created, translated in the German versions as "Elastoman," characterized by the ability to distort his body in every conceivable way, as if it were made of rubber.

In a more recently released horror comedy called simply "Rubber" (2010, directed by Quentin Dupieux), a car tire comes to life and kills animals and people with its psychokinetic energy. Eventually, the tire is shot and torn, but it comes to life again as a tricycle and recruits other tires. This movie is another example of how rubber stimulates the imagination. This is easily explainable.

Rubber seems to stand in the middle as a material between the world of the inorganic and the world of the living. It appears dead and alive at the same time, and that makes it not only fascinating but also a little scary. It has a skin-like feel, is warm to touch, and above all it reacts in a decidedly lively and even alive-like way, such as when pressure is applied, much like with living things. It does not simply accept distortions, but reacts to them. Its movements, its jumping, and its wriggling have a peculiar physiognomy.

Perhaps the quasi-living, the middle position between the living and the dead, the organic and the inorganic, is connected with another quite special feature of rubber products. For these have an eroticizing effect on some people. The striking, intense smell of rubber products seems to play a considerable role in this (Anonymous, 2018). Rubber dresses, which fit the body like a second skin and can also be polished to a high shine, are suitable for transformation games. The constricting effect of the material may play a role in its eroticizing effect as it can strangulate, leading one to sweat underneath, which are unpleasant sensations in themselves but may also have a positive effect in erotic contexts. For many years, there have been magazines and journals and hundreds if not thousands of videos aimed exclusively at rubber fetishists. And, of course, companies manufacture corresponding products.

Even famous authors occasionally write about rubber fetishism, as the section about a plastics factory called IG Farben in Thomas Pynchon's novel *Gravity's Rainbow* shows. Here, too, the special smell of rubber plays an important role

(Pynchon, 1973, pp. 487–488).[4] In science, rubber fetishism seems to have received little attention so far. Research does not seem to have gone beyond individual case studies in the psychoanalytical context (Bohne & Lehrndorfer, 1955, also Mitscherlich, 1983).

The paradoxical combination of robustness and elasticity is probably the most decisive factor in the use of rubber in technical and industrial contexts. Rubber is extremely hard-wearing and solid, with a smooth, waterproof and nonslip surface. Yet it can be stretched in all directions. It almost appears to have its own memory! These properties make rubber well-suited to mediating between hard, technical structures, similar to the way tendons and muscles in the body are connected to bones, making the body mobile. Rubber industrialist Paul W. Litchfield, then president of Goodyear Tire & Rubber, drew this comparison as early as 1939: "Think of our industrial structure as a living thing, the skeleton of which is composed of metal and cement, the arterial system of which carries a life stream of oil, and the flexing muscles and sinews of which are of rubber" (Tully, 2011, p. 17).

Within the field of technology, rubber is therefore often what tendons and muscles are to the human body. Rubber is also the skin of many technical structures. Many tools, for example hammers and screwdrivers, have rubber handles that make them easier to hold, ensuring that they fit well in the hand and are easy to grip. A rubber grip prevents the hand from slipping. Just as the insides of our hands and feet, due to the well-known microstructure of the skin, the so-called papillary ridges, are smooth but not slippery, rubber surfaces are characterized by the fact that they provide grip. It is not without reason that even today the soles of shoes are made of rubber. But rubber is not only used where slipping is to be prevented. Like a skin, rubber also seals technical structures from the outside. Moreover, it does not conduct electricity; rubber is a so-called insulator. It is waterproof and airtight, resistant to many acids and alkalis, and is hardly ever attacked by aggressive substances. It can therefore also be used to seal certain technical structures.

The ubiquity of rubber in our world obscures the fact that it was not always available. Rubber has a long and eventful history. Rubber – or *caoutchouc* – is, in fact, perhaps the most extraordinary and important new material to have become known in Europe since the discovery of metals. Rubber is one of the new materials whose mass use is associated with the technological modernization of industry since the nineteenth century. It spread rapidly throughout Europe from the middle of the nineteenth century and subsequently enabled

---

[4] In the episode narrated by "Greta," a fantasy material called "imipolex" plays the central role in the erotic imagination. The reference to butadiene (p. 487) makes one think of synthetic rubber since it is made from butadiene by polymerization.

increasingly widespread motorization (rubber was essential for tire production; for context regarding the motorization of road traffic, see Merki, 2002) and electrification (rubber is used as an electrical insulator). Given its wide range of applications, it is not surprising that rubber or *caoutchouc* attracted general attention on the occasion of the Great Exhibition in London in 1851. In the second half of the nineteenth century, rubber was one of the most sought after commodities in Europe, and natural rubber remained one of the most important basic materials for modern industrial production until the late 1940s when it became possible to produce it synthetically from coal and limestone. Rubber only lost its status as an "icon of industrial modernity" with the development of new, fully synthetic materials from the 1950s onwards. Nevertheless, rubber is still one of the most important strategic materials today, with production increasing every year.

About half of annual rubber production comes from natural raw materials, that is, mostly from the milk of the *Hevea brasiliensis*, while half is synthetically produced. The highly industrialized processes that are used to produce virtually all rubber products in use today often lead us to forget that rubber is not a European invention.

7 Rubber Histories and the Representation of Indigenous Peoples of South and Central America

Without rubber, we would live in a different world in which not only the rubber duck, the rubber boot, or the condom would be missing but also the car, the airplane and the bicycle, for whose tires the majority of rubber is produced and used. Almost all inventions of the industrial revolution were (and are) dependent on rubber, from the steam engine, which would not work without rubber seals, to the railroad, which needed rubber brakes, to almost all electrical machines and devices, which need rubber (or today, rubber substitutes) as an insulator. It is not surprising, therefore, that there are also many histories and stories about rubber:

> Perhaps no other substance has had as much historical information written about it as rubber. From the early use of natural rubber in the pre-Columbian era and subsequent discovery, experimentation and development of rubber into an industry, to the synthesis of a substitute in the 20th century, there have been many aspects to the evolution of one of mankind's most important materials (Long, 2001, p. 493).

With these words a special bibliography on the history of rubber begins, which includes 255 titles. There are indeed quite a few historical accounts of rubber, and today the list could probably be doubled or tripled. Very many of these accounts share common features. Yet when it comes to the non-European prehistory of rubber, one hardly encounters original information based on a study of primary sources; instead, one finds rather questionable generalizations. This in itself would not be significant, nor even surprising, if it was not for the fact that these generalizations are all rather similar. This point will be critically revised in this section by focusing on Indigenous uses of rubber and the inventions they led to.

Let us recall a typical account of the story of rubber. It can be found in Stefan Zweig's work *Brazil: Land of the Future* which first appeared in 1941 and which is still being reprinted today. Here, Zweig portrays rubber as coffee's competitor. The latter was "the economic king of Brazil":

> The pretender [to the crown] is rubber. Its demands are justified by a certain moral right; for, unlike coffee, it is not a newly arrived immigrant, but a native citizen. The rubber tree, *Hevea brasiliensis*, was originally found in the forests of the Amazon. Three hundred million of these trees have been growing there for hundreds and hundreds of years without their peculiar shape and precious juice having been discovered by Europeans. On his journey to the Amazon in 1736, La Condamine is the first to notice that the natives sometimes used the trees' liquid resin to make their sails and vessels waterproof. But this sticky resin cannot be exploited industrially, as it has no resistance to high and low temperatures; and only a small amount of it ... [is] used in primitively made articles ... A decisive turn, however, is brought about by Charles Goodyear's discovery that a sulphur alligation changes the soft material into a new one less sensitive to heat and cold. With one stroke, then, rubber becomes one of the "Big Five" great necessities of the modern world, hardly less important than coal, oil, timber and ore. Rubber is needed for tubes and galoshes; and after the invention of the bicycle and the automobile its uses take on gigantic proportions. (Zweig, 1941, pp. 116–117)

What do we learn about rubber in these lines? The Indigenous peoples of South and Central America had only produced primitive and instable objects that did not resist high or low temperatures. Their rubber goods are therefore described as "primitively made articles." It was Goodyear, then, who turned the material into a completely new one "with one stroke"; having left its problems behind, rubber could now nurture hopes for the "throne" of the "economic king of Brazil."

This passage is representative of many similar ones found in fictional and nonfictional literature on rubber. In one of the most famous rubber narratives, Vicki Baum's internationally successful novel *The Weeping Wood* (Baum, 1944), made up of several different independent narratives, the stereotype of the useless, smelly, and sticky material from the jungle is depicted even more dramatically. Here, in a broadly described fictional scene, a Jesuit of German origin gives an indigenous boy the order of making rubber shoes with the help of clay molds, which the boy then does. But at the decisive moment, the material turns out to be sticky and thus hardly usable. The rubber demonstration fails and the Jesuit's superior says: "Well, I do not think this substance is fit for use among civilized people. I prefer to leave it to the savages for making their toys" (Baum, 1944, p. 29).

In this scene, Indigenous rubber technology is reduced to the simple practice of letting latex trickle over the feet in order to obtain rubber shoes. The use of clay molds would then have been devised by a wise European (a German, of course), but due to an error on the part of the Indian helper, this alleged innovation does not lead to success. Here again, as elsewhere in Vicki Baum's work, the actual inventors of rubber are portrayed as helpless children. In the same novel, a few pages further on, it is Charles Goodyear who, as nearly always, is portrayed as the hero and the martyr of rubber (Baum, 1944, ch. 2). The absurd exaggeration of Goodyear's achievement corresponds with the complete devaluation, even misjudgment, of the cognitive and technical achievement of the Indigenous peoples who in truth not only discovered the rubber tree but also invented a very sophisticated and effective rubber technology, as we will see in Sections 10 and 11.

What seems remarkable about these "Indians," according to Vicki Baum, is their love of poetry. An epigraph at the start of her novel reads: "The Amazon Indians who discovered the rubber tree long before America was discovered, called it Cahuchu or Cauchu, which means: The Weeping Wood" (Baum, 1944). Again, the Amazonian Indians are portrayed as being very simple people who come up with beautiful names that again express their naiveté. Vicki Baum takes her etymology of the word *cahuchu* or *cauchu* from the botanist W. H. Johnson (1909, p. 1), which still circulates today in the literature on rubber (see, for example, Tully, 2011, p. 20). There is not the slightest evidence for this etymology, despite its presence even in scientific literature. What we know is that the etymology of the word *Cauchuc* (Cobo, 1964, p. 268) or *Cahuchu* (La Condamine, 1745, p. 68) cannot be clarified; we do not even know for certain from which language it originated. One plausible and quite obvious etymology is that suggested by Julius Platzmann. He assumes it originated from *Tupí* and claims that rubber means "tree resin" (Platzmann, 1901, p. 376). Georg Friederici (1934, pp. 145–146), on the other hand, has collected evidence that supports its Peruvian origin from the word *caucho*, showing that it appeared in a Khetschua dictionary as early as 1613 with the meaning "sorcerer (*encantador*)." In the United States and England, however, people speak of (Indian) rubber, in memory of a discovery popularized by Joseph Priestley, which probably goes back to the instrument maker *Edward*

Nairne. According to Priestley, Nairne had discovered that pencil drawings could be rubbed out better with rubber cubes than with the previously used bread dough.

Histories of rubber, whether written by professional historians or, as is often the case, by rubber chemists or rubber technicians, often contain stereotypical elements when it comes to describing the preindustrial history of rubber. For example, even the American historian Michael Edward Stanfield, in a book that focuses on the exploitation of Indigenous peoples, writes that the rubber that the Indians invented had downsides that were only overcome by Anglo-American inventors: "But rubber presented some problems, too. Its texture and elasticity changed with temperature: it became hard and brittle in the cold, and soft and tacky in the heat. During the first half of the nineteenth century, Europeans and Americans intensified their effort to stabilize or 'improve' rubber" (Stanfield, 1988, p. 20). John Tully, another historian, also repeats the same narrative pattern in his work *The Devil's Milk: A Social History of Rubber* (Tully, 2011). He explains: "There were, however, serious drawbacks with Indian rubber, or caoutchouc, as it was still widely known. It was sticky and smelly in temperate conditions, melted in heat, and when cold or aged, it became brittle" (Tully, 2011, p. 37). Once again, it is Charles Goodyear who brings about the dramatic turnaround in this narrative:

> In 1839, working in his improvised laboratory, Goodyear found that if rubber was mixed with sulfur at high temperatures it was radically metamorphosed and could stand extremes of heat and cold without melting or cracking. The process also did away with the atrocious odor, which had deterred potential customers from purchasing rubber goods. In effect, Goodyear had created a new substance from raw rubber (Tully, 2011, p. 40).

This periodization of rubber history is questionable in part because the core of Goodyear's invention, the use of sulfur to improve the properties of rubber, was already well-known at this time; it had been described in the widely used chemistry textbook of Jöns Jacob Berzelius, (1838, p. 106f., see also Lüdersdorff, 1832). But, furthermore, this way of telling rubber's history totally neglects the high standard of Indigenous rubber technology and rubber artifacts.

If we compare a larger number of rubber histories, we will find that the following narrative elements are repeated again and again:

(1) The names *cahuchu* or *caoutchouc* and the like, which were used to refer to rubber in the past, are repeatedly attributed to a "poetic" Indigenous name that means "tears of the tree" (or "the weeping tree" or "flowing wood").

(2) The ritual ball games of the Maya and Aztecs in Central America, where rubber balls were used, are referred to. It is always mentioned that the balls

were made of solid rubber, that they were bounced with the hips, and that the games frequently involved human sacrifice.

(3) It is pointed out that the material used by the Indians was made known to Europeans by the French mathematician and Amazonian traveler Charles-Marie de la Condamine in the eighteenth century.

(4) Most authors turn to the nineteenth century and note that jungle rubber was indeed a special material insofar as it was elastic, malleable, and impermeable to water, but it was hardly usable because it became sticky when hot and brittle when cold. It was only thanks to the process known by the dramatic name "vulcanization," developed by Charles Goodyear, that the imperfect substance from the jungle became a great material, subsequently used industrially on a large scale. As technically gifted and inventive people, as experts, the Indigenous peoples of Amazonia do not appear in this narrative (only in three rubber histories that I know of are some pages to be found devoted to Indigenous skill and knowledge: Forbin, 1943, Giersch & Kubisch, 1995, and Serier, 1993).

(5) The rest of the story is then usually written into the plot of the "triumphal march" of vulcanized rubber, which is bumpy, with ups and downs as well as downsides. Rubber is often referred to as "king" and thus placed alongside other "kings," that is, other materials of global economic importance.

It is therefore evident that the role of Indigenous peoples is narrated in a rather stereotypical manner. The well-known double-sided representation of childlike paradisiacal naiveness and barbaric cruelty in sacrificial rituals is often invoked, and this still shapes the European representation of Indigenous peoples of South and Central America today (Müller, 1995, pp. 19–20). This inaccurate representation conceals the fact that the Indigenous peoples of South and Central America, very many of whom did not survive the encounter with Europeans, possessed considerable inventiveness and technical competence and that the knowledge they developed and handed down through the generations was probably more important to the development of European and American industry than all the gold and silver that was looted or extorted. Today, the global rubber industry generates annual sales in the double-digit billions.

I would therefore like to correct the standard narrative in the following respects. First, I would like to focus on the role assigned to Indigenous knowledge. The chemical and general technical competence of the Indigenous peoples of the Americas (Nordenskiöld, 1929, p. 284, see also Nordenskiöld, 1918, pp. 80–84, Nordenskiöld, 1930, pp 1–124, and Hosler, Burkett, &

Tarkanian, 1999) will be appreciated more thoroughly than is typically the case in the literature. Such competence is evidenced by the highly developed metallurgical practices in some places (Hosler, 2009) and by the important plants, such as corn, cassava, cocoa, and peanuts, as well as many other highly important pharmaceutical substances such as pilocarpine (Pinheiro, 1997), curare, cocaine, and quinine (Gänger, 2021), which were discovered and used for the first time by Indigenous peoples.

To the contrary of what is often said about it, Indigenous rubber technology was very complex and produced excellent rubber products, and therefore it has considerable importance to the history of rubber. A whole new history of rubber thus emerges that is not only driven by a concern for greater fairness but also for telling exciting new stories. I then turn to the question of the material traces of rubber and how its life continues after it has been discarded after use. This is where old tire landfills come into view as well as fine dust and microplastics. From these traces of industrial rubber, I then take a final look back at the advantages of Indigenous rubber technology.

8 Indigenous Knowledge

Almost all studies so far devoted to rubber have been concerned with the production of knowledge by European or North American technicians or chemists (see, for example, the excellent study by Streb, 2004). The concept of Indigenous knowledge, on the other hand, has only recently received attention in the history of technology and science (Safier, 2010). There are some studies on the transfer of such knowledge to Europe and beyond (Schiebinger 2004); however, not much research has been undertaken in an attempt to characterize it. Yet the concept of Indigenous knowledge is indispensable if laboratory-related material histories are to be expanded on and if, in addition to scientific knowledge, *nonscientific knowledge* is also to be taken into consideration.

Indigenous knowledge belongs to nonscientific knowledge and is even a particularly prominent type of it. Such knowledge has been thematized in international law since about the mid 1980s (Carneiro da Cunha, 2009, pp. 10–26, see also Antweiler, 1998). It concerns the knowledge of Indigenous communities or Indigenous peoples, meaning that of the peoples or communities that settled in a particular region earlier than later arrivals. The term is therefore relative. Indigenous communities and peoples exist worldwide, including in Europe, Asia, and Australia. In this context, however, the term applies to those peoples who lived (and still live) in the Americas before European colonization.

Their knowledge can be quite clearly described as autonomous because it was formed in isolation from European and Asian exchange.

Of course, today there is a continuous contact, and probably the vast majority of Indigenous communities in the Americas are now in intensive exchange with the rest of the world. Nevertheless, the notion of Indigenous knowledge is indispensable as a historical concept, as the history of rubber shows. The term (Li, 2007, p. 16f.) refers to knowledge that Indigenous peoples have of materials, plants, animals, technical processes, and natural phenomena. Even though this knowledge is usually referred to as traditional (Carneiro da Cunha, 2009, p. 28, also Agrawal, 1995 and Antweiler, 1998), it can be assumed that it is not static but rather dynamic in the sense that it develops through individual discoveries and inventions which are then adopted or imitated by others (Tarde, 2009, pp. 110–129).

In principle, Indigenous knowledge is likely to emerge in a similar way to Western scientific knowledge, namely, through observation, trial and error, logical reasoning, analogy, chance, and so on. Moreover, in some cases it is plausible that the hitherto little-noticed observation of animal behavior (Newton & Wolfe, 1992) is not insignificant for the emergence of this knowledge. Undeniably important is also the often discussed transfer of technical practices from one field to another (Leroi-Gourhan, 1992b, pp. 344–345).

Indigenous knowledge, as has been said, is not as static as the term "traditional" might suggest, but it is unlikely to be as dynamic as knowledge in European scientific culture. This is because scientific knowledge, as has been widely shown, owes its dynamism to the fact that it is written down and circulated in print form and thus transformed through constant circulation and exchange produced by organized collectives of specialized researchers (Totzke, 2004, pp. 79–85).

Unfortunately, we have very few modern ethnological field studies on Indigenous chemical knowledge (Silva, 2000, also Castelló Iturbide, 1972). Therefore, it is hard to make even any general remarks about it. However, it can be assumed that Indigenous knowledge is not organized in theory because scientific theory presupposes writing. Such knowledge is therefore likely to be situational rather than abstract, additive rather than subordinate, and probably organized primarily through narrative.

According to the classical European legal conception, such knowledge was common property, which meant it could be used by anyone, especially by Europeans, without further ado. It is only today that work is being done on the legal regulations for dealing with such traditional knowledge, coordinated by the World Intellectual Property Organization, a UN specialized agency based in Geneva. In what follows, we are not concerned with the rights that, according to more recent views, should be observed in the use of traditional knowledge or with the question of whether such rights should have been observed in the past. Here, the focus is on further characterizing Indigenous knowledge so that we are able to more accurately grasp its role in the history of rubber.

Only *material Indigenous knowledge* will be considered here as this aspect was highly relevant to European knowledge, which is not true to the same extent of the spiritual aspects of Indigenous knowledge. Indeed, it was primarily the knowledge of Indigenous peoples about the tangible and visible aspects of their environment that was important to European colonizers. Their spiritual knowledge, on the other hand, was considered somewhat problematic. As is well-known, in the course of missionary efforts Indigenous spiritual knowledge was to be replaced with the spiritual beliefs of European colonizers.

In relation to rubber, the material knowledge of Indigenous peoples had the following elements: first, Indigenous people knew which plants yielded latex, where to find them, and how and when to extract the latex, the rubber milk, without harming the tree. This is the botanical and biogeographical component of Indigenous knowledge of rubber. They also knew how to treat the milk with a certain smoking process so that objects made from it remained stable and did not, for example, turn to rot or become sticky in the heat. This is the chemical component of their knowledge. Finally, they knew how to make useful products from it and invented a variety of very specific rubber products whose industrially manufactured descendants are still in use around the world today. This is the technical component of Indigenous rubber knowledge.

The chemical dimension of Indigenous knowledge is crucial. This concerned knowledge of a method for preserving manufactured rubber products so that they did not decay. This dimension of Indigenous rubber knowledge is obviously particularly important because a rubber product that quickly becomes brittle or even rots has very limited usefulness. Yet it is precisely this aspect of Indigenous rubber knowledge that is totally ignored in many modern rubber histories, as Stefan Zweig's example (see Section 7) shows.

One may raise the objection that terms such as "knowledge" or even expressions such as "chemical," "botanical," or "technical" are of European origin and that Indigenous understandings of the world cannot be adequately reconstructed using such terms. Yet to banish terms such as Indigenous (chemical, technical, botanical) knowledge from rubber histories because of methodological concerns results in narratives that emphasize only the importance of European and North American science and technology. Indigenous peoples appear in these histories only as "primitive peoples" who invent poetic names ("tears of the tree") or as victims of cruel persecution, but not as competent actors. Historiography is in particular danger of being biased and of consciously or unconsciously placing itself in the service of a particular group of the living (Harth, 1996, e.g., pp. 833–837). A Eurocentric history of materials that focuses only on European scientific knowledge runs the risk of prolonging colonial mentalities and perceptions, thus making itself a participant in the exploitation of Indigenous inventions without hardly a thought given to respect, gratitude, or even reciprocity. At the same time, it narrows the horizon because it excludes from the outset highly interesting ways of dealing with substances and materials, namely, those that are not carried out in laboratories but rather in forests under an open sky, where one does not work with test tubes but rather with the equipment that is available at hand in the forest. And yet, even in this way, very sophisticated technical processes and material transformations are possible.

9 Indigenous Rubber Products

High-bouncing rubber balls first introduced Europeans to the amazing properties of rubber, as mentioned earlier. However, as the reports of early travelers in South and Central America show, rubber was used in far more diverse and creative ways. It was used, for example, to produce enemas. This involved the lost mold process, in which the product was molded around a clay core. A sandy clay was used for this purpose, which could easily be crushed again inside the formed rubber bottle and washed out through an opening. A hollow bird bone was then placed on top of the bottle formed in this way, which served as a cannula. Thus, enemas were produced and, as reported by the French naturalist de la Condamine of the Omagua, they were passed around before feasts in order to give the invited guests relief and to create space for the ingestion of the food and drink to be consumed (de La Condamine, 1745, p. 79f.). Hallucinogenic substances were also applied through such enemas; smaller syringes, on the other hand, were used to snort hallucinogenic substances through the nose (Veigl, 1785, p. 87).

The technical originality of these elastic syringes compared to the European equivalents is known to all travelers who have reported on them. Rubber enemas have the advantage of allowing self-treatment (Krünitz, 1789, p. 82f.). The syringes prompted Europeans to create their own medical products such as hand pumps for injections and milk suckers, among other things. Such rubber products are still in use today. There were also other medical applications that seemed rather novel. Rubber strips, for example, were used by the Couna in Darién province on the border of Colombia as a mouthguard, pushed between the teeth of fever patients to prevent them from grinding them during their convulsions (Forbin, 1943, p. 12).

It is only a small step from the rubber bottle to the hollow ball (and vice versa), since only the opening has to be closed (Nordenskiöld, 1918, p. 85). Ball games with a hollow or solid ball were not only known to the Maya and the Aztecs but also played throughout tropical South America, as many travel reports show (Roosevelt, 1926, p. 159; further descriptions have been compiled by Nordenskiöld, 1918, and also Gumilla, 1745, p. 190f.; a photo of the game at the Paressi-Kabisi is shown by Schmidt, 1914, p. 183).

Furthermore, wide rubber bands such as foils and mats were produced, which could be used to make various objects waterproof when they were wrapped in them (Martius, 1867, p. 440); shoes and waterproof rubber-coated textiles and bottles were also made (Barrère, 1743, pp. 139–141). Indigenous peoples also used rings made of rubber as jewelry and for bundling branches together, among other things. Today, rubber bands are available in every supermarket and are well-known companions of everyday life. Cornelius Pauw writes in his *Recherches philosophiques* that such rings were used by some Indigenous peoples as penis rings to increase sexual pleasure (Pauw, 1777, p. 54). If this holds true, Indigenous people not only pioneered syringes, rubber boots, raincoats, and waterproof mats, but also the large market in rubber sex toys. However, very little is known about this; neither is it known whether condoms were already in use among Indigenous peoples. It seems at least possible.

What is certain, however, is that many children's toys were made of rubber. The rubber duck or the rubber alligator corresponding to it was originally an Indigenous invention. The latex was cast in molds for this purpose; hollow play dolls were also made (Krünitz, 1789, p. 82). Furthermore, rubber was used as tinder and for torches that shone brightly (Martius, 1867, p. 440 and Wavrin, 1941, p. 179). The Jivaros used rubber as an incendiary device in warfare, throwing pieces of ignited rubber at rooftops during attacks (Wavrin, 1941, p. 103).

Even though the Indigenous peoples of Amazonia invented neither the eraser nor the car tire, it is evident that a very large proportion of modern rubber products were invented by them and adopted by the Europeans after they became acquainted with Indigenous products through overseas trade. In any case, it was important that the things made from rubber remained as stable as possible. Rubber poses special problems, as we have seen. But what we have not seen hitherto is that the Indigenous peoples knew how to solve these problems with an autonomous and efficient technology. It is in this context that we encounter the chemical dimension of Indigenous knowledge of rubber.

10 Problems of Untreated Rubber

Rubber stimulates the imagination: countless things can be made from it. But rubber also has its problems. Let us hear from Friedrich Lüdersdorff, one of the first chemists who published on rubber. He says that light can cause a serious transformation in rubber. If a rubber product is exposed to daylight:

> decomposition begins after a short time. In the thinnest parts [the rubber] is attacked first; it takes on the impressions of the fingers, and the lines of the skin remain permanently visible on it . . . . This state of change increases more and more, and soon extends through the whole mass, which now passes into the second stage. This is a complete stickiness, which becomes more and more prevalent, and brings the mass into a state of deliquescence . . . . The third and last stage is finally . . . initially superficial, but then deepened drying, which results from the formation of a hard skin, which increases in thickness more and more . . . the decomposition is [now] finished. [The rubber] is now just as brittle and fragile as it used to be pliable and elastic. (Lüdersdorff, 1832, p. 34f.)

In addition, untreated rubber is very sensitive to microbial infestation. Rubber goods can literally rot, as we have already seen and as an American rubber historian vividly describes:

> It was during the winter of 1832 that Goodyear passed the New York store of the Roxbury Company. Wearing a ragged coat, and a blacksmith's leather apron for additional warmth, he made his momentous visit to the rubber works, and met proprietor Chaffee. Chaffee welcomed him, and confided the bad news that his goods were going "sour". It was true. Rubberized cloth was literally rotting in warehouses: Chaffee had actually buried $20,000 worth of it to keep it off the market. (Wilson, 1943, p. 44, see also p. 46)

The main method used in a contemporary context to deal with these problems is to allow sulfur to react with rubber. The use of sulfur was first published in detail by Lüdersdorff in 1832 (Lüdersdorff, 1832, p. 62). His idea was made internationally known by the already mentioned seventh volume of Jöns Jakob Berzelius' textbook of chemistry, which was translated into German and French and widely used (Berzelius, 1838, p. 106f., see also Eck, 1832 and Hayward, 1865, p. 7).

The use of sulfur was taken up by Charles Goodyear, who was presumably inspired directly or indirectly (via Nathaniel Hayward) by Lüdersdorff: Goodyear heated the rubber–sulfur mixture and thus made the use of sulfur more efficient. By combining this with the masticating roller invented by Thomas Hancock (Coates, 1987, pp. 22–28 and 37–42), a process was then developed whose basic features are still practiced today. The heroic term "vulcanization," coined by William Brockedon and then adopted by Hancock and finally also by Goodyear (Coates, 1987, p. 38f.), suggests not a gradual qualitative improvement, but an abrupt change that led to a universally applicable material that subsequently started its "triumphal march around the world." Goodyear himself still used the term "metallic gum-elastic" in 1839 (Lunn, 1952, p. 23).

Even contemporary histories of rubber, as I have mentioned, tell rubber's story in such a way as to suggest that the Indigenous material would have remained useless if European or American inventors had not "cured" it through vulcanization. What is true, however, is that European and American inventors developed their own processes that solved the problems of rubber and made it possible to produce durable rubber products both from fresh latex – that is, the sap supplied by *Hevea brasiliensis* and other plants – and from dried latex. However, the view that Europeans and North Americans were the first and only ones to succeed in this is wrong. This widespread periodization and perspectivization of the history of rubber requires correction. For one thing, even contemporary rubber products are not made for eternity. They do their job, but they are still, as everybody knows, subject to becoming sticky or brittle after being exposed to sunlight or heat for long periods of time. Indigenous rubber technology and rubber chemistry was sophisticated enough to deal with well-known problems associated with rubber. In fact, the Indigenous peoples of South America invented a type of organic vulcanization, and it was only because this invention was made many centuries ago somewhere in Amazonia that the history of rubber got off the ground at all. If Europeans had not seen functional and stable rubber products, they would never have written such enthusiastic praise of this "miraculous" substance.

Indeed, Indigenous people had their own chemical process that stabilized rubber and made it robust against heat, sunlight, and germination. Sulfur plays no role in this process; it is extremely rare in the Amazonian lowlands. But sulfur is not essential; there is never just one solution to a particular technical problem. It is possible to stabilize rubber without sulfur in such a way that its desirable properties, can be maintained for a very long time. And here is the point where we must take a closer look at the material of rubber and its transformations, where our study has to include knowledge of chemistry and knowledge of substances and their transformations. The process is in principle well-known. It is based on fumigation. Smoking is a common technique around the world that is used primarily to preserve meat and fish but also dairy products. In Indigenous rubber technology, this well-known process is transformed in an ingenious way. It is applied to a material that is not a foodstuff. As a rule, thin layers of liquid are applied to clay molds and then held in the smoke. The smoke causes the water to evaporate, and the substances contained in the smoke react, transform, and stabilize the resulting rubber layer. Among other substances, smoke contains strong antibiotics, which is the reason why fish or meat can be preserved with it. All these compounds are in a chemical sense organic compounds, as opposed to sulfur, which is an inorganic substance. Organic vulcanization works; the smoke also protects the rubber from rotting and from growing mold. It is the same principle that protects smoked ham. In addition, the accumulated soot particles protect the rubber from atmospheric oxygen and UV light. The elasticity of the product is also improved (for more detail on the chemistry, see Soentgen, 2013, especially pp. 316–319).

This fumigation process provided a functional equivalent to European vulcanization. The Indigenous products did not have the problems I have described, and this is the only explanation for the fact that rubber was in use everywhere. After all, there would have been no use for a sticky product in Amazonia either. That the Indigenous process was effective is shown by, among other things, the fact that it is still used today, both in its original form – smoked rubber sheets are still traded on the world market – as well as by the fact that soot is still added to rubber because it makes it resistant to solar radiation, as every black rubber car tire or bicycle tire shows.

To clarify, what I mean by a "functional equivalent" is a technical process that solves the perceived problems of a material at a historical time as satisfactorily as an alternative contemporary technique. A functional equivalent is not a makeshift but an effective technical solution. It fixes the problem, which is exactly what the sophisticated Indigenous process for fumigating rubber did. Many competent authors (Geer, 1922, p. 9) who had had the opportunity to work with these products acknowledged the high quality of Indigenous rubber goods. Goodyear himself paid detailed tribute to Indigenous products in his own promotional literature and did not believe that his own achievements could replace them everywhere. He claimed that despite their imperfections, Indigenous rubber products, even without all the improvements he himself developed, are "almost indispensable to man" (Goodyear, 1939, p. 23). "The bottles, shoes, and toys made of it [i.e. native gum] by the Indians of Para, were exceedingly useful" (Goodyear, 1939, p. 23). Similarly enthusiastic are the statements of Henry Wickham, best known for his illegal export of 7,000 seeds of *Hevea brasiliensis* to London, which broke the Brazilian monopoly. His judgment was based on solid knowledge. In his opinion, only Indigenous goods were able to withstand the rigors of the forest, while European goods quickly degraded and became useless (Wickham, 2012/ 1908, p. 30, see also p. 57).

> That the antiseptic smoke-cure is, and will prove to be, the true method for insuring the production of a rubber retaining the characteristic quality of strength and durability under wear and tear and atmospheric variation, together with the important point of being homogeneous and of even quality throughout, I am convinced. It certainly does not seem to have been remembered that certain of the forest Indian tribes of tropical America, for instance, the Guayangomo and other, have from a time long anterior to the incursion of the Spaniard, been in the habit of making rubber goods for their own use – such as the beautifully-made quiver-covers for their Warali poison darts, and of a quality for strength and durability excelling any European factory-made. In fact, European factory-made rubber perishes so rapidly in these equatorial forests as to become quite soon useless. (Wickham, 2012/1908, p. 30)

Accordingly, until the middle of the nineteenth century, there was an international wholesale trade in Indigenous rubber products from Pará in the western Amazon (Schidrowitz & Dawson, 1952, p. XIII) that would probably never have arisen if the Indigenous products had not been solid and stable (Cruz, 1964, pp. 81–83).

How does Indigenous rubber technology work, in detail? The latex sap is dried and chemically transformed over a smoldering fire of young twigs and urucarí nuts (from the palm *Attalea excelsa*) or Inajá nuts, which are burned together (these nuts are obtained from the palm *Attalea maripa*, other palm nuts also seem to have been used; for more information, see Wickham, 2012/1908, p. 31).

A book on rubber written in 1851 describes the Indigenous process on the river island of Gurupá in the Amazon Delta:

> A fire is made on the ground of the seed of nuts of a palm-tree, of which there are two kinds: one called urucarí, the size of a pigeon's egg, though longer; and the other inajá, which is smaller. An earthen pot, with the bottom knocked out, is placed, mouth down, over the fire, and a strong pungent smoke from the burning seeds comes up through the aperture in the bottom of the inverted pot. The maker of the rubber now takes his last, if he is making shoes, or his mold, which is fastened to the end of a stick; pours the milk over it with a cup, and passes it slowly several times through the smoke until it is dry. He then pours on the other coats until he has the required thickness; smoking each coating until it is dry. Moulds are made either of clay or wood; if of wood, it is smeared with clay, to prevent the adhesion of the milk. When the rubber has the required thickness, the moulds are either cut out or washed out. (Herndon, 1853, pp. 326–327; see also Sioli, 2007, pp. 91–93)

Another traveler describes how the decorations were applied:

> You will, moreover, notice a number of Indian girls (some very pretty) engaged in making various impressions, such as flowers &c., upon the soft

surface of the rubber, by means of their thumb nails, which are especially pared and cultivated for this purpose. After this final operation, the shoes are placed in the sun to harden, and large numbers of them may be seen laid out on mats in exposed situations (Warren, 1851, p. 17).

Henry Pearson, the editor of *India Rubber World*, a magazine on rubber goods, the rubber trade and the rubber industry, reports that the particular smell of smoke from the nuts in the forest indicated the rubber collectors' camps from afar (Pearson, 1911, p. 68). The process was therefore quite odor-intensive and undoubtedly harmful to health. But it fulfilled its material purpose; it 'cured' the rubber from its 'diseases' like rotting, molding, getting brittle etc. Fumigation is the core component of the Indigenous production technique; this technique corresponds to a special know-how as well as a know-that. The process succeeded in achieving the essential goals of any rubber technology: that is, durability of molded objects and increased elasticity. It did so by using operations and raw materials that were readily available in the rain forest. Indigenous rubber technology was thus an optimal technical solution to a problem, adapted to a specific production environment since it used the available resources – latex, clay, and fire – to create a product that remained stable and was even exported in the eighteenth and nineteenth centuries. Today, goods produced in this way would still be exported if an alternative method of stabilization had not been developed that allowed Europeans and North Americans to produce their own goods.

In addition to the commonly used fumigation method, there were apparently other Indigenous techniques, although not quite as efficient. In 1999, Hosler and her colleagues showed in a fascinating, much-quoted study that latex harvested from *Castilla elastica* (a tree growing in Central America that was used by the Aztecs and Maya) was mixed with sap from *Ipomoea alba*, a variety of the showy vine that is popular as an ornamental plant, causing coagulation of the latex. At the same time, the elastic properties of the resulting rubber were improved (Hosler, Burkett, & Tarkanian, 1999).

Yet the Mesoamerican processing technique, which Hosler and her colleagues brought to light, had only a very local distribution and depended on plants that cannot be found everywhere in South and Central America. In contrast, Amazonian organic vulcanization, as it might be called, is independent of any special plant; even the nuts can be replaced, green branches are sufficient. It was used nearly everywhere where rubber goods were produced. Even today, as I have said, it is still of importance as a pre-treatment in rubber technology.

11 The Place of Indigenous Knowledge in the History of Rubber

Indigenous knowledge, to stress this point again, was important to the history of rubber in at least three ways. First, Indigenous biogeographical knowledge about where to find the latex-bearing plants, and how and when best to tap them, was significant. Second, the diverse range of products invented by Indigenous peoples was important. This demonstrates how the extraordinary properties of rubber could be transformed into practically useful products. Many if not all of these product ideas, such as rubber shoes, rubber toys, rubber rings, raincoats, and so on, were adopted by European and North American industry. Third, Indigenous knowledge of efficient methods of stabilizing and protecting rubber against rapid spoilage by rot, heat, or sunlight are of central importance to the entire history of rubber. It is true that the process of smoking was substituted by the invention of sulfur – vulcanization. Sulfur was readily available everywhere in industrialized regions of Europe and North America, quite unlike in Amazonia.

With their own rubber technology, based on a organic method of stabilizing the polymer, Europeans and North Americans emancipated themselves from Indigenous knowledge and began to develop their own rubber knowledge and empire. European rubber research culminated in the first half of the twentieth century with the invention of an industrial rubber synthesis, which made it possible not only to work with rubber on an industrial scale but to produce rubber from scratch, that is, from raw materials such as coal and lime in any quantity (Soentgen, 2017). Today, synthetic rubber accounts for about 60 percent of worldwide consumption. Nevertheless, Indigenous technologies are by no means completely displaced, as latex is still collected not only from plantations but also from wild or semiwild forests. Smoking is also still in use as a pretreatment and leads to the so-called smoked sheets that smell like bacon.

The development of an autonomous European–North American knowledge of rubber had strong repercussions for the Indians who, as a consequence, no longer appeared as competent producers of finished goods. They were now only important as procurers of raw materials and thus in a far more subordinate role. It was no longer the *quality* of their products, guaranteed by their *knowledge* of the material, that came into play, but rather the *quantity* of the delivered material itself. The treatment of Indigenous peoples changed accordingly, as did representations of them in European and American rubber historiography.

To summarize this account: Indigenous rubber technology by no means constituted the naive use of a natural product that owed its existence to the rich tropical flora. Such an account would naturalize what in reality was a cultural achievement. Rather, this technology is owed to Indigenous cognitive and technical inventions that were culturally passed on over the centuries from one generation to another. One can very well speak of "high tech" in the sense of a *highly developed* technology because a series of precisely coordinated procedures was required from latex extraction to the finished product. Indigenous rubber technology is therefore a great and highly intelligent cultural achievement.

This can be seen even more clearly when we consider that, theoretically, rubber could have been discovered in the "Old World" as well. The botanical prerequisites for such a discovery were available since latex-bearing plants (and mushrooms) also exist in Europe, Africa, and Asia. A total of about 2,000 latex-bearing species are known worldwide, of which quite a few are suitable for latex extraction and rubber production, but this was not known until Europeans came into contact with Indigenous rubber products. For example a certain species of dandelion with the botanical name *Taraxacum kok-saghyz*, which grows in Kazakhstan and China, has a relatively high latex content. However, nobody used its sap until Indigenous products from South America demonstrated what could be done with it. The fact that rubber was not invented in Asia but in South America underscores the technical ingenuity and expertise of the Indigenous peoples who first used rubber, who recognized the value of its discovery, who culturally passed on and refined the associated technology, and who invented new products (Nordenskiöld, 1929, p. 279).

The Indigenous peoples of South and Central America not only possessed functional equivalents to vulcanization, they also invented efficient processing methods and applications of the material that went far beyond rubber balls. By efficient processing methods I mean methods that (1) lead to working products and (2) are adapted to the production environment in the sense that they use what is there. If we embark on this trail, we also expand our understanding of chemistry, for we come across chemical practices that, even though they do not require a retort or a test tube or purified and standardized chemicals, are amazingly effective and lead to convincing results.

Thus, if we extend our study of rubber, and follow it beyond the factory floors and laboratories to the forests and villages from where it originally came, we finally discover a new field of research in transnational history and in the history of science and technology. Chemistry in the open air, a chemistry without test tubes and Erlenmeyer flasks, is a largely unknown field when it comes to the chemical practices employed. The importance of Indigenous ingenuity when it comes to the example of rubber is shown when we leave behind the traditional realms of chemical history research in journals, textbooks, and laboratories. Beyond these cultural spaces, other cultural practices and knowledge systems are found that have interacted with scientific knowledge.

Material history research fits well with overarching trends in contemporary historical research and research in the area of the environmental humanities. Here, one should not only think of the history of knowledge but also of the reassessment of transnational history that is currently much discussed in Western historical scholarship, in which a one-sided representation that only pays attention to the achievements and initiatives of Europeans is being overcome (Chakrabarty, 2000, also Wendt, 2016, e.g. pp. 11–21).

Indigenous rubber technology is therefore not just an exotic curiosity. On the contrary, it is fundamental to the history of rubber. It cannot be attributed to an individual inventor. It is not even possible to identify with any certainty which Indigenous people first succeeded in this invention, although several sources single out the Omagua, once very numerous in Amazonia, for their developed and effective rubber technology. In any case, organic vulcanization, which was probably first introduced somewhere in Amazonia in prehistoric and certainly in pre-Columbian times, is the most important invention in the *entire history* of rubber simply because all later discoveries, even sulfurvulcanization, depended on it. Without this invention, rubber would never have become the subject of European or American research and technology, or at least not until much later. American and European industrialization would have taken a different path, with important products such as the bicycle, the automobile and even the airplane probably remaining rather marginal because without shock-absorbing rubber tires, they would not have become efficient modes of transportation.

The knowledge invested in Indigenous rubber technology and Indigenous rubber products exemplifies a high level of problem-solving ability. It decisively tamed the problematic tendencies of rubber to become sticky and brittle with the substances and means available in the forest and exploited its extraordinary properties to create a wide variety of products, all of which are still, without exception, on the market today.

12 Rubber and Rubbish: Tire Dumps and Microrubber

We have looked at the history of rubber and how it developed. We considered how rubber appears everywhere in contemporary life and the stories that are told about it. We compared these stories with the oldest accessible records and discovered the almost unknown and even hidden realm of Indigenous rubber technology. We tried to understand that technology chemically, developing a new, polyphonic and more reflective history of rubber. Now we are approaching the end of the story – of this story. We have already heard that materials have long lives. Rubber products are no exception since they do not cease to exist when they are no longer used or usable; they do not melt into the air; they hang around even after they have long been discarded.

Where does all the rubber go? On highways, here and there, facilities are installed to collect the rainwater that runs off the highway in order to treat it in such a way as to retain the rubber residues in it. These everyday observations are not irrelevant because by far the largest share (70 percent) of global rubber production – 27.3 million tons in 2016 – is used to make car tires (Halsband et al., 2020).

Is tire wear on roads problematic? We see black skid marks everywhere. We know that microrubber accounts for a certain fraction of the dust in cities. Is this microrubber harmful? Due to numerous additives, industrially produced rubber products cannot be reintegrated into the ecological cycle; furthermore, they are sometimes downright toxic. Such rubber is a complex mixture. In order to optimize its functionality and durability as a commodity, certain metal and organic compounds are integrated into it, which are toxic in larger quantities. You can smell the difference when you set alight an Indigenous-made rubber product; such products are still available to buy today in many cities along the Amazon. They give off nothing more than an aromatic smell, very similar to the smell of resinous wood. While this smell may not be healthy in larger quantities, it is at least not as toxic as the acrid smoke that is produced when you burn an industrially produced household rubber band.

Now, the smoke emitted by such industrially produced rubber products may not be a quality criterion since such products are not manufactured to be burned. But rubber products, as we have seen, do leave their mark; they leave skid marks on the roads and are also often dumped as waste at the end of their lives. So they end up in the environment – and with them the whole cocktail of chemicals they contain, many of which can have adverse impacts on human health. Since old tires are often dismantled and shredded to make surfaces for sports pitches, for example, the substances contained in them can find their way into our environment and eventually into our bodies.

Industrially produced vulcanized rubber is so greatly transformed chemically in order to make it more durable and robust that it is practically no longer biodegradable. It is therefore a contributor not only to microrubber but also to so-called microplastics (Tamis et al., 2021). In fact, a considerable part of microplastics is nothing other than tire fragments (Kole et al., 2017, also Root, 2023). A great proportion of macrorubbish and microrubbish is industrially produced rubber. It is well-known that microplastics pollute waterways and have a harmful effect on aquatic organisms that devour the small, indigestible particles. Such particles enter our bodies through the city air we breathe and the water we drink, as well as through our consumption of fish and sea salt. It is only very recently that tire manufacturers have taken responsibility for the problem and have come to offer tires that are supposed to contain at least *fewer* toxic ingredients.

The products manufactured by the Indigenous peoples of South and Central America did not have these problems. Their products might be described as *sustainable polymers*, not least because they were (and sometimes still are) produced exclusively from renewable raw materials, whereas industrially produced rubber always involves considerable consumption of fossil fuel-based raw materials which is why industrial rubber production, especially the production of synthetic rubber, contributes considerably to global warming with production processes emitting large amounts of carbon dioxide into the atmosphere.

Indigenously produced rubber products, as we have seen, may not be quite as durable as industrially produced rubber products that are optimized with the aid of sulfur and other additives. However, against the backdrop of the problem of microplastics (Hale et al., 2020), it becomes clear that this somewhat lower performance and resistance is not always and in any regard a disadvantage. As modern rubber products do not decompose and quite often contain toxic substances, the problem of microplastics increases every year. Rubber products produced through Indigenous methods, on the other hand, contain no heavy metals, sulfur, or persistent organic compounds. Therefore, they neither poison the environment nor our bodies at the end of their lives. They become brittle and then rot, not unlike how resin from a tree rots.

Much effort has been expended in cultural studies on deconstructing the "ecological Indian" (Krech, 1999, also Stephenson, 2012). However, perhaps scholars have been a little too eager in their criticism. It is true that Indigenous peoples also transformed their environment and perhaps even caused the extinction of certain species, but there is a great difference between *their* destructive tendency and that of contemporary industrial societies. Such differences should not be ignored. Indigenous communities were much more ecological and lived a much more sustainable lifestyle than we do. They did not bring about a global ecological crisis. We have. Their material culture was not only full of technical creativity but was also much more sustainable. Almost all Indigenous-produced products were compostable. This also applies to Indigenous rubber in contrast to the optimized and thus often ecotoxic industrially produced rubber, which does not degrade easily.

Rubber is not an isolated example of this. Indigenous sweeteners are likewise consistently biodegradable, such as the extracts from *Stevia rebaudiana* (Soejarto, Addo, & Kinghorn, 2019), which were called Caa-he-eh by the

Guarani in Paraguay (Fawcett, 1953, p. 114) and are now consumed worldwide. Such substances do not pose a threat to the environment. That might sound self-evident, but biodegradability is *not* a feature of synthetic sweeteners. As can be seen from saccharin, the oldest (Merki, 1993) and still most widely used synthetic sweetener, synthetic substances are extremely persistent and therefore accumulate in groundwater (Pang, Borthwick, & Chatzisymeon, 2020). It may only be used in tiny quantities per application, but billions of tiny quantities can have a considerable impact.

The result is that the material culture of traditional Indigenous peoples can be described as being comparatively more sustainable than ours. It has been shown many times over that the ground surfaces of our contemporary world are often poisoned, with urban soils containing numerous toxic substances in high quantities, including many toxic heavy metals (Biasioli, Barberis, & Ajmone-Marsan, 2006). Such urban soils are therefore unsuitable for agricultural use. In contrast, the soils on which Indigenous peoples settled are characterized by increased and almost permanent fertility. They do not contain any toxic heavy metals. In Amazonia, these soils are referred to as Indigenous black soils (*terra preta do indio*) and are often cultivated for crops. Recent research has shown that these soils act as a permanent carbon sink, and there is currently a lot of research being conducted on how to produce such soils on a large scale in order to mitigate global warming (Hilbert et al., 2017). This example is another indication that Indigenous material culture entailed significantly fewer ecological problems than the material culture of Western industrial societies. It is not yet foreseeable whether one day a way will be found to produce biodegradable – maybe even compostable and thus more environmentally friendly – rubber products in a similar way to the Indigenous peoples of Amazonia. Yet there has been a certain revival of Indigenous rubber technologies in Amazonia (Center for International Forestry Research, 2004).

If we look back on our journey through the histories of rubber, we started with a well-known companion of everyday life. We looked at the stories that are told about this companion and analyzed them. We focused especially on the role of Indigenous inventions and their representations in popular and even academic histories of rubber. Relying on firsthand experience, extant relics of the Indigenous rubber technology, and elder travel reports, we identified certain stereotypes in the popular rubber histories. Now we can say that it is wrong to see nothing but primitiveness and inferiority in the technical solutions and inventions of Indigenous peoples. The rubber products they produced were creative and efficient technical solutions to problems. They developed consistent and efficient and even sustainable technological procedures that were optimally adapted to a specific production environment. That is high tech in the best sense of the word. Such products also have advantages over the sophisticated industrially produced rubber products because they are, by far, better integrated into ecological cycles than industrially produced rubber products, which create permanent problems through their contribution to the buildup of microplastics in the soil and in water bodies at the end of their life cycle. Just as Indigenous rubber products fascinated the participants in Christopher Columbus' first voyages, they could well continue to inspire the future of the rubber industry, and hence the history of rubber.

All in all, this Element, focused on Indigenous knowledge in material histories, hopefully convinced the reader that the field of material histories is a fascinating and promising area of research.

References

Agrawal, A. (1995). Dismantling the Divide between Indigenous and Scientific Knowledge. *Development and Change*, 26(3), p. 413–439.

Anonymous. (1857). The Invention of Vulcanized India Rubber. *Scientific American*, 12(22), p. 173.

Anonymous. (2018). My Life in Sex: "My Rubber Fetish Has Enriched My Life." *Guardian* (September 21). https://bit.ly/49xUxIj (last accessed: January 14, 2024).

Antweiler, C. (1998). Local Knowledge and Local Knowing: An Anthropological Analysis of Contested "Cultural Products" in the Context of Development. *Anthropos*, 93(4), pp. 469–494.

Antweiler, C. (2022). *Anthropologie im Anthropozän: Theoriebausteine für das 21. Jahrhundert*. Darmstadt: wbg Academic.

Appadurai, A. (1986). *The Social Life of Things: Commodities in Cultural Perspective*, 1st ed. Cambridge: Cambridge University Press.

Augustinus, A. (1962). De vera religione. In K.-D. Daur, ed., *Corpus Christianorum Series Latina, Vol. XXXII: Aurerlii Augustini Opera Pars IV, I.* Turnholt: Brepols Editores Pontificii, pp. 169–260.

Barrère, P. (1743). *Nouvelle Relation de la France Equinoxiale*. Paris: Piget and Durand.

Bartolovich, C. (2017). Unobtainium. In Imre Szeman, ed., *Fueling Culture: 101 Words for Energy and Environment*. New York: Fordham University Press, pp. 357–360. https://doi.org/10.1515/9780823273935-097.

Baum, V. (1944). *The Weeping Wood*. Garden City, NY: Doubleday, Doran & Company.

Bensaude-Vincent, B., Loeve, S., Nordmann, A., & Schwarz, A. (eds.). (2017). *Research Objects in Their Technological Setting*. London: Routledge.

Berzelius, J. J. (1838). *Lehrbuch der Chemie*, Vol. VII, 4th ed. Dresden: in der Arnoldischen Buchhandlung.

Biasioli, M., Barberis, R., & Ajmone-Marsan, F. (2006). The Influence of a Large City on Some Soil Properties and Metals Content. *Science of the Total Environment*, 356(1), pp. 154–164.

Billerbeck, M. & Zubler, C. (2000). *Das Lob der Fliege von Lukian bis L. B. Alberti: Gattungsgeschichte, Texte, Übersetzung und Kommentar*. Bern: Peter Lang.

Blackwell, M. (2007). *The Secret Life of Things: Animals, Objects, and It-Narratives in Eighteenth-Century England*. Lewisburg, PA: Bucknell University Press.

Bohne, G. & Lehrndorfer, G. (1955). Zwei Fälle von Gummi-Fetischismus. *Nervenarzt*, 26(7), pp. 280–285.

Böschen, S. (2000). *Risikogenese: Prozesse gesellschaftlicher Gefahrenwahrnehmung – FCKW, DDT, Dioxin und Ökologische Chemie*. Opladen: Leske+Budrich.

Carneiro da Cunha, M. (2009). *"Culture" and Culture: Traditional Knowledge and Intellectual Rights*. Chicago, IL: Prickly Paradigm Press.

Castelló Iturbide, T. (1972). Maque o Laca. *Artes de México*, 153, pp. 33–81. www.jstor.org/stable/24317086 (last accessed: January 14, 2024),

Center for International Forestry Research. (2004). Rubber, Vegetal Leather. In *Riches of the Forest: Fruits, Remedies and Handicrafts in Latin America*, pp. 97–100. www.jstor.org/stable/pdf/resrep02039.30 (last accessed: January 14, 2024).

Chakrabarty, D. (2000). *Provincializing Europe: Postcolonial Thought and Historical Difference*. Princeton, NJ: Princeton University Press.

Chakraborty, P. (2000). Science, Nationalism, and Colonial Contestations: P. C. Ray and His Hindu Chemistry. *Indian Economic and Social History Review*, 37(2), pp. 185–213.

Chang, H. (2012). *Is Water H_2O? Evidence, Realism and Pluralism*. Vol. 293 of the series Boston Studies in the Philosophy and History of Science. Dordrecht: Springer.

Chang, H. & Jackson, C. (2007). *An Element of Controversy: The Life of Chlorine in Science, Medicine, Technology and War*. Vol. 13 of the BSHS Monograph series. London: British Society for the History of Science.

Clarenbach, A. (2002). *Finis libri: Der Schriftsteller und Journalist Heinrich Eduard Jacob (1889–1967)*. PhD dissertation, University of Hamburg. https://ediss.sub.uni-hamburg.de/handle/ediss/3561 (last accessed: July 6, 2023).

Coates, A. (1987). *The Commerce in Rubber: The First 250 Years*. New York: Oxford University Press.

Cobo, B. (1964). *Historia del Nuevo Nundo*. Bibliotheca de Autores Espanoles, Vol. 91, Sects. 1–439 (Books 1–10). Madrid: Atlas.

Coslovsky, S. V. (2006). The Rise and Decline of the Amazonian Rubber Shoe Industry: A Tale of Technology, International Trade and Industrialization in the Early 19th Century. Massachusetts Institute of Technology, Working Paper No. 39. https://bit.ly/3IFCTXa.

Cronon, W. (1992). A Place for Stories: Nature, History and Narrative. *Journal of American History*, 78(4), pp. 1347–1376.

Cruz, E. (1964). *História da Associação Comercial do Pará: Centenário de sua fundação 1864–1964*. Belém: Universidade do Pará.

De La Condamine, C.-M. (1745). *Relation abrégée d'un voyage fait dans l'intérieur de l'Amérique méridionale*. Paris: Veuve Pissot.

De Ridder, M. (2000). *Heroin: Vom Arzneimittel zur Droge*. Frankfurt: Campus.

Dewey, J. (1925). *Experience and Nature*. Vol. I of Lectures upon the Paul Carus Foundation. Chicago, IL: Open Court Publishing Company.

Douglas, A. (1995). *Uneasy Sensations: Smollett and the Body*. Chicago, IL: University of Chicago Press.

Eck, L. (1832). Friedrich Wilhelm Lüdersdorff. *Gummi-Zeitung*, 32, pp. 967–968.

Emeis, S. & Schlögl-Flierl, K. (2021). *Phosphor: Fluch und Segen eines Elements*. Munich: oekom.

Ertl, G. & Soentgen, J. (ed.) (2015). *N. Stickstoff – ein Element schreibt Weltgeschichte*. Munich: oekom.

Espahangizi, K. (2014). Stofftrajektorien: Die kriegswirtschaftliche Mobilmachung des Rohstoffs Bor, 1914–1919 (oder: was das Reagenzglas mit Sultan Tschair verbindet). In Kijan Espahangizi, Barbara Orland, & Sabine Baier, eds., *Stoffe in Bewegung: Beiträge zu einer Wissensgeschichte der materiellen Welt*, 1st ed. Zürich: Diaphanes, pp. 173–208.

Fawcett, P. H. (1953). *Exploration Fawcett*. London: Hutchinson.

Feinberg, K. R. (2012). *Who Gets What: Fair Compensation after Tragedy and Financial Upheaval*. New York: Public Affairs.

Fernández de Oviedo, G. (1992/1535). *Historia General Y Natural de las Indias*, 1st ed. Madrid: Atlas.

Festa, L. (2015). It-Narratives and Spy Novels. In P. Garside & K. O'Brien, eds., *The Oxford History of the Novel in English: Volume 2 – English and British Fiction 1750–1820*, 1st ed. Oxford: Oxford University Press, pp. 335–352.

Forbin, V. (1943). *Le Caoutchouc dans le Monde*. Paris: Payot.

Forster, E. M. (1969). *Aspects of the Novel*. London: Edward Arnold Publishers.

Friederici, G. (1934). Lehnwörter exotischer Herkunft in europäischen Sprachen. *Zeitschrift für französische Sprache und Literatur*, 58(3/4), pp. 135–155.

Friederici, G. (1960). *Amerikanistisches Wörterbuch und Hilfs-Wörterbuch für den Amerikanisten*, 2nd ed. Hamburg: de Gruyter.

Gadamer, H.-G. (1995). *Gesammelte Werke: Vol. X – Hermeneutik im Rückblick*. Tübingen: Mohr.

Gänger, S. (2021). *A Singular Remedy: Cinchona across the Atlantic World, 1751–1820*. Cambridge: Cambridge University Press.

Geer, W. C. (1922). *The Reign of Rubber*. London: Allen & Unwin.

Geyer, R., Jambeck, J. R., & Law, K. L. (2017). Production, Use, and Fate of All Plastics Ever Made. *Science Advances*, 3(7), p. e170078. https://doi.org/10.1126/sciadv.1700782.

Gibson, J. J. (1979). *The Ecological Approach to Visual Perception*. Boston, MA: Houghton Mifflin.

Giersch, U. & Kubisch, U. (1995). *Gummi: Die elastische Faszination*. Berlin: Nicolai.

Goodyear, C. (1939). Gum-Elastic and Its Varieties, with a Detailed Account of Its Applications and Uses, and of the Discovery of Vulcanization. In C. Goodyear and T. Hancock, eds., *A Centennial Volume of the Writings of Charles Goodyear and Thomas Hancock*. Boston, MA: American Chemical Society, pp. 1–379.

Gumilla, J. (1745). *El Orinoco Ilustrado y Defendido, Historia Natural, Civil, y Geographica De este Gran Rio, y de Sus Caudalosas Vertientes*, Vol. I. Madrid: Manuel Fernandez.

Haines, C. R. (ed.) (1919). *The Correspondence of Marcus Cornelius Fronto with Marcus Aurelius Antoninus, Lucius Verus, Antoninus Pius, and Various Friends*, Vol. 1. London: William Heinemann.

Hale, R. C., Seeley, M. E., La Guardia, M. J., Mai, L., & Zeng, E. Y. (2020). A Global Perspective on Microplastics. *Journal of Geophysical Research: Oceans*, 125(1), p. e2018JC014719. https://doi.org/10.1029/2018JC014719.

Halsband, C., Sørensen, L., Booth, A. M., & Herzke, D. (2020). Car Tire Crumb Rubber: Does Leaching Produce a Toxic Chemical Cocktail in Coastal Marine Systems? *Frontiers in Environmental Science*, 8. https://doi.org/10.3389/fenvs.2020.00125.

Hamp, P. (1936). *L'oeuvre: La peine des hommes – Marée fraiche, Vin de Champagne*, 5th ed. Paris: Gallimard.

Harth, D. (1996). Geschichtsschreibung. In Gert Ueding, ed., *Historisches Wörterbuch der Rhetorik Online*, Vol. III. Ebook. Tübingen: Niemeyer and de Gruyter. https://doi.org/10.1515/hwro.

Haumann, S., Roelevink, E.-M., Thorade, N., & Zumbrägel, Chr. (ed.) (2023). *Perspektiven auf Stoffgeschichte: Materialität, Praktiken, Wissen*. Bielefeld: transcript.

Hayward, N. (1865). *Some Account of Nathaniel Hayward's Experiments with India Rubber, Which Resulted in Discovering the Invaluable Compound of That Article with Sulphur*. Norwich, CT: Bulletin Job Printing Office.

Heidegger, M. (1927). *Sein und Zeit: Erste Hälfte*. Halle: Niemeyer.

Herndon, L. (1853). *Exploration of the Valley of the Amazon Made under the Direction of the Navy Department.* Washington, DC: Robert Armstrong.

Hilbert, K., Soentgen, J., Von Groote-Bidlingmaier, C., Herzog-Schröder, G., Pabst, E., & Timpf, S. (2017). Terra preta de índio: Commodification and Mythification of the Amazonian Dark Earths. *Gaia*, 26(2), pp. 136–143.

Hoefer, J. C. F. (1866). *Histoire de la chimie*, Vol. II, 2nd ed. Paris: Didot.

Hoppe, B. (1979). *Aus der Frühzeit der chemischen Konstitutionsforschung: Die Tropanalkaloide Atropin und Cocain in Wissenschaft und Wirtschaft.* Munich: Oldenbourg.

Hosler, D. (2009). West Mexican Metallurgy: Revisited and Revised. *Journal of World Prehistory*, 22(3), pp. 185–212. https://doi.org/10.1007/s10963-009-9021-7.

Hosler, D., Burkett, S. L., & Tarkanian, M. J. (1999). Prehistoric Polymers: Rubber Processing in Ancient Mesoamerica. *Science*, 284(5422), pp. 1988–1991.

Huppenbauer, M. & Reller, A. (1996). Stoff, Zeit und Energie: Ein transdisziplinärer Beitrag zu ökologischen Fragen. *Gaia*, 5(2), pp. 103–115.

Jacob, H. E. (1934). *Sage und Siegeszug des Kaffees: Die Biographie eines weltwirtschaftlichen Stoffes.* Berlin: Rowohlt.

Jacob, H. E. (1998). *Coffee: The Epic of a Commodity.* Short Hills, NJ: Burford Books.

Janich, P. (2001). *Logisch-pragmatische Propädeutik: Ein Grundkurs im philosophischen Reflektieren*, 1st ed. Weilerswist: Velbrück Wissenschaft.

Johnson, W. H. (1909). *The Cultivation and Preparation of Para Rubber.* London: Crosby, Lockwood and Son.

Jung, M. (2014). *Gewöhnliche Erfahrung.* Tübingen: Mohr Siebeck.

Kantorowicz, E. (1957). *The King's Two Bodies: A study in Mediaeval Political Theology.* Princeton, NJ: Princeton University Press.

Kepler, J. (1611). Strena seu de nive sexangula. *The Latin Library.* www .thelatinlibrary.com/kepler/strena.html (last accessed: January 14, 2024).

Kole, P., Löhr, A. J., van Belleghem, F. G. A. J., & Ad Ragas, M. J. (2017). Wear and Tear of Tyres: A Stealthy Source of Microplastics in the Environment. *International Journal of Environmental Research and Public Health*, 14(10), pp. 1265. https://doi.org/10.3390/ijerph14101265.

Köller, W. (2006). *Narrative Formen der Sprachreflexion: Interpretationen zu Geschichten über Sprache von der Antike bis zur Gegenwart.* Berlin: de Gruyter.

Kondylis, P. (1999). *Das Politische und der Mensch: Grundzüge der Sozialontologie.* Berlin: Akademie-Verlag.

Kopp. H. (1843–1847). *Geschichte der Chemie*, Vols. I, III, & IV. Braunschweig: Vieweg.

Krech, S. (1999). *The Ecological Indian: Myth and History.* New York: Norton.

Krünitz, J. G. (1789). *Oekonomische Encyklopaedie oder allgemeines System der Staats-, Stadt-, Haus- u. Landwirthschaft, und der Kunst-Geschichte*, Vol. 22. Berlin: Pauli.

Las Casas, B. de (1971). *Los indios de México y Nueva España: Antología.* México City: Editorial Porrúa.

Leroi-Gourhan, A. (1992a). *Evolution et techniques*, Vol. I: *L'homme et la matière.* Paris: Michel.

Leroi-Gourhan, A. (1992b). *Evolution et techniques*, Vol. II: *Milieu et technique.* Paris: Michel.

Levi, P. (1975). *Il sistema periodico.* Turin: Einaudi.

Li, X. (2007). Overcoming Market Failure and Rationalizing Traditional Indigenous Medicinal Knowledge Protection Regimes: An Economic Approach and Case Study in China. Unpublished PhD thesis, University of St. Gallen, Switzerland.

Long, J. C. (2001). The History of Rubber: A Survey of Sources about the History of Rubber. *Rubber Chemistry and Technology*, 74(3), pp. 493–508.

Lüdersdorff, F. (1832). *Das Auflösen und Wiederherstellen des Federharzes, genannt: Gummi elastikum – Zur Darstellung luft- und wasserdichter Gegenstände.* Berlin: J. W. Boite.

Lunn, R. W. (1952). Vulcanization. In P. Schidrowitz & T. R. Dawson, eds., *History of the Rubber Industry: Compiled under the Auspices of the Institution of the Rubber Industry.* Cambridge: Heffer, pp. 23–39.

Marks, L. (2001). *Sexual Chemistry: A History of the Contraceptive Pill.* New Haven, CT: Yale University Press.

Marschall, L. (2008). *Aluminium: Metall der Moderne.* Munich: oekom.

Martini, E. A. (2012). *Agent Orange: History, Science, and the Politics of Uncertainty.* Amherst, MA: University of Massachusetts Press.

Martius, C. F. P., von (1867). *Beiträge zur Ethnographie und Sprachenkunde Amerika's zumal Brasiliens: Erster Band – Zur Ethnographie Amerikas zumal Brasiliens.* Leipzig: Fleischer.

Marty, B. & Monin, H. (2003). *Le premier âge de l'and: Histoire d'une molécule de l'hérédité.* Paris: Vuibert.

Meikle, J. L. (1995). *American Plastic: A Cultural History.* New Brunswick, NJ: Rutgers University Press.

Merki, C. M. (1993). *Zucker gegen Saccharin: Zur Geschichte der künstlichen Süßstoffe.* Frankfurt: Campus.

Merki, C. M. (2002). *Der holprige Siegeszug des Automobils, 1895–1930: Zur Motorisierung des Straßenverkehrs in Frankreich, Deutschland und Schweiz*. Wien: Böhlau.

Mitscherlich, A. (1983). Aus der Analyse eines Gummi-Fetischisten. *Psyche*, 37(10), pp. 867–904.

Mizrahi, V. (2014). Sniff, Smell, and Stuff. *Philosophical Studies: An International Journal for Philosophy in the Analytic Tradition*, 171(2), pp. 233–250. www.jstor.org/stable/24704128 (last accessed: January 14, 2024).

Müller, W. (1995). *Die Indianer Amazoniens: Völker und Kulturen im Regenwald*. Munich: C. H. Beck.

Neer, R. M. (2013). *Napalm: An American Biography*. Cambridge, MA: The Belknap Press of Harvard University Press.

Newton, P. & Wolfe, N. (1992). Can Animals Teach Us Medicine? *British Medical Journal*, 305(6868), pp. 19–26.

Nordenskiöld, E. (1918). Om Indianernes Anvendelse af Gummi i Sydamerika. *Geografisk Tidsskrift*, 24, pp. 80–84.

Nordenskiöld, E. (1929). The American Indian as an Inventor. *Journal of the Royal Anthropological Institute of Great Britain and Ireland*, 59, pp. 273–309.

Nordenskiöld, E. (1930). *Modifications in Indian Culture through Inventions and Loans*. Gothenburg: Erlanders.

Pang, L., Borthwick, A. G. L., & Chatzisymeon, E. (2020). Determination, Occurrence, and Treatment of Saccharin in Water: A Review. *Journal of Cleaner Production*, 270, article 122337. https://doi.org/10.1016/j.jclepro.2020.122337.

Pankau, J. G. (1994). Erzählung. In G. Ueding, ed., *Historisches Wörterbuch der Rhetorik*, Vol. II. Tübingen: Niemeyer & de Gruyter, pp. 1432–1438.

Partington, J. R. (1960). *A History of Greek Fire and Gunpowder*, 1st ed. Cambridge: Heffer.

Pauw, C., de (1777). *Recherches Philosophiques sur Les Américains*, Vol. I. Berlin: Decker.

Pearson, H. C. (1911). *The Rubber-Country of the Amazon: A Detailed Description of the Great Rubber Industry of the Amazon Valley*. New York: The India Rubber World.

Pfeiffer, W. (1993). *Etymologisches Wörterbuch des Deutschen*, Vol. II, 2nd ed. Berlin: Akademie-Verlag.

Pinheiro, C. U. B. (1997). Jaborandi (*Pilocarpus* sp., rutaceae): A Wild Species and Its Rapid Transformation into a Crop. *Economic Botany*, 51(1), pp. 49–58.

Platzmann, J. (1901). *Das Anonyme Wörterbuch Tupi-Deutsch und Deutsch-Tupi.* Leipzig: B. G. Teubner.

Pretel, D. & Camprubí, L. (2018). Technological Encounters. Locating Experts in the History of Globalization. In D. Pretel & L. Camprubí, eds., *Technology and Globalization: Networks of Experts in World History.* Cham: Springer International Publishing, pp. 1–26.

Pynchon. T. (1973). *Gravity's Rainbow.* New York: Viking Press.

Reller, A. (2013). *Ressourcenstrategien: Eine Einführung in den nachhaltigen Umgang mit Ressourcen.* Darmstadt: Wissenschaftliche Buchgesellschaft.

Reller, A., Bublies, T., Staudinger, T., et al. (2009). The Mobile Phone: Powerful Communicator and Potential Metal Dissipator. *Gaia,* 18(2), 127–135.

Repohl, M. (2023). Die Beziehungsqualität der materiellen Welt: Perspektiven einer weltbeziehungssoziologischen Analyse von Materialität. Unpublished PhD dissertation, University of Erfurt.

Richardson Jr., W. H. (1858). *The Boot and Shoe Manufacturers Assistant and Guide: Containing a Brief History of the Trade.* Boston, MA: Higgins, Bradley & Dayton.

Ricoeur, P. (1984). *Time and Narrative,* 2nd ed. Chicago, IL: Chicago University Press.

Roosevelt, T. (1926). *Through the Brazilian Wilderness and Papers on Natural History.* Vol. V of *The Works of Theodore Roosevelt.* New York: Scribner.

Root, T. (2023). Tires: The Plastic Polluter You Never Thought About. *National Geographic* (September 20). www.nationalgeographic.com/environment/article/tires-unseen-plastic-polluter (last accessed: January 14, 2024).

Roth, P. (2021). Gottfried Wilhelm Leibniz über die Entdeckung des Phosphors. In S. Emeis & K. Schlögl-Flierl, eds, *Phosphor: Fluch und Segen eines Elements.* Munich: oekom, pp. 41–54.

Ruthenberg, K. (2022). *Chemiephilosophie.* Berlin: de Gruyter.

Safier, N. (2010). Global Knowledge on the Move: Itineraries, Amerindian Narratives, and Deep Histories of Science. *Isis,* 101(1), pp. 133–145.

Sarasin, P. (2011). Was ist Wissensgeschichte? *Internationales Archiv für Sozialgeschichte der deutschen Literatur,* 36(1), pp. 159–172.

Schapp, W. (1959). Philosophie der Geschichten. Leer: Rautenberg.

Schlaudt, O. (2021). Müll-Philosophie: Des Teufels Staub und der Engel Anteil. *Merkur,* 870, pp. 5–16.

Schmidt, M. (1914). Die Paressi-Kabisi. *Baessler-Archiv,* 4, pp. 167–250.

Schwarz, A. (2019). Sir, Perhaps Some Perrier in your Benzene? *Forbes* (April 23). https://bit.ly/3Tqmw7a (last accessed: January 14, 2024).

Scheerbart, P. (2012). Lesabéndio: An Asteroid Novel. New York: Wakefield.

Schidrowitz, P. & Dawson T. R. (eds.) (1952). *History of the Rubber Industry: Compiled under the Auspices of the Institution of the Rubber Industry.* Cambridge: Heffer.

Schiebinger, L. (2004). *Plants and Empire: Colonial Bioprospecting in the Atlantic World.* Cambridge, MA: Harvard University Press.

Schilling, L. & Vogel, J. (2019). *Transnational Cultures of Expertise: Circulating State-Related Knowledge in the 18th and 19th Centuries.* Berlin: de Gruyter & Oldenbourg.

Semper, G. (1878). *Der Stil in den technischen und tektonischen Künsten oder praktische Aesthetik: Erster Band – Textile Kunst.* Munich: Bruckmann.

Serier, J.-P. (1993). *Histoire du Caoutchouc.* Paris: Editions Desjonquères.

Silva, F. A. (2000). As tecnologias e seus significados: Um estudo da Ceramica dos Asuriní do Xingu e da cestaria dos Kayapo-Xikrin sob uma perspectiva etnoarqueologica. Unpublished PhD dissertation, University of São Paulo. www.teses.usp.br/teses/disponiveis/8/8134/tde-03122013-165920/pt-br.php (last accessed: January 14, 2024).

Simon, C. (1999). *DDT: Kulturgeschichte einer chemischen Verbindung.* Basel: Christoph-Merian-Verlag.

Sioli, H. (2007). *Gelebtes, geliebtes Amazonien: Forschungsreisen im brasilianischen Regenwald zwischen 1940 und 1962.* Munich: Pfeil.

Smil, V. (2013). *Making the Modern World: Materials and Dematerialization,* 1st ed. Hoboken, NJ: Wiley.

Soejarto, D. D., Addo, E. M., & Kinghorn, A. D. (2019). Highly Sweet Compounds of Plant Origin: From Ethnobotanical Observations to Wide Utilization. *Journal of ethnopharmacology,* 243. https://doi.org/10.1016/j.jep.2019.112056.

Soentgen, J. (1997). *Das Unscheinbare: Phänomenologische Beschreibungen von Stoffen, Dingen und fraktalen Gebilden.* Berlin: Akademie-Verlag.

Soentgen, J. (2006). Bio, Transfair und mehr: Die Kaffeewelt seit den 1950er bis heute. In A. Reller, J. Soentgen, & H. E. Jacob, eds., *Kaffee: Die Biographie eines weltwirtschaftlichen Stoffes.* Munich: oekom, pp. 315–348.

Soentgen, J. (2008). Stuff: A Phenomenological Definition. In K. Ruthenberg & J. van Brakel, eds., *Stuff: The Nature of Chemical Substances.* Würzburg: Königshausen & Neumann, pp. 71–91.

Soentgen, J. (2013). Die Bedeutung indigenen Wissens für die Geschichte des Kautschuks. *Technikgeschichte,* 80(4), pp. 295–324.

Socntgen, J. (2014). *Atome und Bücher: Primo Levis Erzählung Kohlenstoff im Periodischen System und Hermann Römpps "Lebensgeschichte eines Kohlenstoffatoms."* Mainz: Johannes Gutenberg-Universität Mainz. http://doi.org/10.25358/openscience-738.

Soentgen, J. (2017). Making Sense of Chemistry: Synthetic Rubber in German Popular Scientific Literature (1929–2009). *Cahiers François Viète*, Vol. III(2). https://journals.openedition.org/cahierscfv/814 (last accessed: January 14, 2024).

Soentgen, J. (2019). *Konfliktstoffe: Über Kohlendioxid, Heroin und andere strittige Substanzen.* München: oekom.

Soentgen, J. (2021). Die Bedeutung alchemistischer Methoden und Ideen für die Entdeckung des Phosphors. In S. Emeis & K. Schlögl-Flierl, eds., *Phosphor: Fluch und Segen eines Elements.* Munich: oekom, pp. 22–40.

Soentgen, J. (2023). The Mobilisation of Matter in the Anthropocene. In S. Zoche, ed., *Blind Date with the Future.* Prinsenbeek: Jap Sam Books, pp. 205–212.

Soentgen, J. & Reller, A. (2009). *CO₂: Lebenselixier und Klimakiller.* Munich: oekom.

Stanfield, M. E. (1998). *Red Rubber, Bleeding Trees. Violence, Slavery, and Empire in Northwest Amazonia, 1850–1933*, 1st ed. Albuquerque, NM: University of New Mexico Press.

Stephenson, B. (2012). On Being "Close to Nature": Identity, Politics, Place. *Time and Mind*, 5(1), pp. 19–31.

Stoff, H. (2023). Vom Wirken zum Stoff zum Wirken. In S. Haumann, E.-M. Roelevink, C. Zumbrägel, & N. Thorade, eds., *Perspektiven auf Stoffgeschichte: Materialität, Praktiken, Wissen.* Bielefeld: transkript, pp. 115–142.

Strawson, P. (1972). *Einzelding und logisches Subjekt (Individuals): Ein Beitrag zur deskriptiven Metaphysik.* Stuttgart: Reclam.

Streb, J. (2004). Der transatlantische Wissenstransfer auf dem Gebiet der Synthesekautschukforschung in Krieg und Frieden: Freiwillige Kooperationen und erzwungene Reparationen (1926–1954). *Technikgeschichte*, 71(4), pp. 283–304.

Tamis, J. E., Koelmans, A. A., Dröge, R., et al. (2021). Environmental Risks of Car Tire Microplastic Particles and Other Road Runoff Pollutants. *Microplastics and Nanoplastics*, 1(10). https://doi.org/10.1186/s43591-021-00008-w.

Tarde, G. (2009). *Die Gesetze der Nachahmung*, 1st ed. Frankfurt: Suhrkamp.

Teissier, P. (2017). From the Birth of Fuel Cells to the Utopia of the Hydrogen World. In B. Bensaude-Vincent, S. Loeve, A. Nordmann, & A. Schwarz, eds., *Research Objects in Their Technological Setting.* London: Routledge, pp.70–86.

Tomarken, A. H. (1990). *The Smile of Truth: The French Satirical Eulogy and Its Antecedents.* Princeton, NJ: Princeton University Press.

Totzke, R. (2004). *Buchstaben-Folgen: Schriftlichkeit, Wissenschaft und Heideggers Kritik an der Wissenschaftsideologie*, 1st ed. Weilerswist: Velbrück.

Tret'iakov, S. (2006). The Biography of the Object. *MIT Magazine*, 118, pp. 57–62.

Tully, J. (2011). *The Devil's Milk: A Social History of Rubber*. New York: Monthly Review Press.

Veigl, F. X. (1785). Gründliche Nachrichten über die Verfassung der Landschaft von Maynas, in Süd-Amerika, bis zum Jahre 1768. In C. G. von Murr, ed., *Reisen einiger Missionarien der Gesellschaft Jesu in Amerika*. Nuremberg: Johann Eberhard Zeh, pp. 1–450.

Veyne, P. (1984). *Writing History: Essay on Epistemology*, 1st ed. Middletown, CT: Wesleyan University Press.

Vogel, J. (2004). Von der Wissenschafts- zur Wissensgeschichte: Für eine Historisierung der "Wissensgesellschaft." *Geschichte und Gesellschaft*, 30(4), pp. 639–660.

Warren, J. E. (1851). *Para; or Scenes and Adventures on the Banks of the Amazon*. New York: G. P. Putnam.

Wavrin, M., de (1941). *Les Jivaros: Réducteurs de Têtes*. Paris: Payot.

Wehling, P. & Böschen, S. (2015). *Nichtwissenskulturen und Nichtwissensdiskurse: Über den Umgang mit Nichtwissen in Wissenschaft und Öffentlichkeit*, 1st ed. Baden-Baden: Nomos.

Wendt, R. (2016). *Vom Kolonialismus zur Globalisierung: Europa und die Welt seit 1500*, 2nd ed. Vol. 2889 of Uni-Taschenbücher. Paderborn: Ferdinand Schöningh.

Westermann, A. (2007). *Plastik und politische Kultur in Westdeutschland*. Zürich: Chronos.

Weyer, J. (1974). *Chemiegeschichtsschreibung von Wiegleb (1790) bis Partington (1790): Eine Untersuchung über ihre Methoden, Prinzipien und Ziele*. Hildesheim: Gerstenberg.

Wickham, H. (2012/1908). *On the Plantation, Cultivation, and Curing of Pará Indian Rubber (Hevea brasiliensis), with an Account of Its Introduction from the West to the Eastern tropics*. Charleston, SC: Nabu Press.

Wilson, C. M. (1943). *Trees and Test Tubes: The Story of Rubber*, 1st ed. New York: Holt.

Zahavi, D. (2019). *Phenomenology: The Basics*. New York: Routledge.

Zemanek, E. (2023). Allheilmittel oder Gift? In E. Zemanek, ed., *Ozon: Natur- und Kulturgeschichte eines flüchtigen Stoffes*. Munich: oekom, pp. 78–105.

Zumbrägel, Chr. (2023). Helium in Bewegung: Flüchtiges Speichern in der Stoff- und Infrastrukturgeschichte (1920–1960). In S. Haumann, F.-M. Roelevink, N. Thorade, & Chr. Zumbrägel, eds., *Perspektiven auf Stoffgeschichte*. Bielefeld: transcript Verlag, pp. 175–206. https://doi.org/10.14361/9783839468944-007.

Zweig, S. (1941). *Brazil: Land of the Future*. New York: Viking Press.

Acknowledgments

I would like to thank the editors, Serenella Iovino, Timo Maran, and Louise Westling; and likewise two reviewers for many very helpful critical remarks on the text and – last but not least – many thanks to Christian Schnurr, Kristy Henderson and to the team of CUP for important comments and suggestions and for copyediting this Element.

Cambridge Elements $\equiv$

Environmental Humanities

Louise Westling
University of Oregon
Louise Westling is an American scholar of literature and environmental humanities who was a founding member of the Association for the Study of Literature and Environment and its President in 1998. She has been active in the international movement for environmental cultural studies, teaching and writing on landscape imagery in literature, critical animal studies, biosemiotics, phenomenology, and deep history.

Serenella Iovino
University of North Carolina at Chapel Hill
Serenella Iovino is Professor of Italian Studies and Environmental Humanities at the University of North Carolina at Chapel Hill. She has written on a wide range of topics, including environmental ethics and ecocritical theory, bioregionalism and landscape studies, ecofeminism and posthumanism, comparative literature, eco-art, and the Anthropocene.

Timo Maran
University of Tartu
Timo Maran is an Estonian semiotician and poet. Maran is Professor of Ecosemiotics and Environmental Humanities and Head of the Department of Semiotics at the University of Tartu. His research interests are semiotic relations of nature and culture, Estonian nature writing, zoosemiotics and species conservation, and semiotics of biological mimicry.

About the Series
The environmental humanities is a new transdisciplinary complex of approaches to the embeddedness of human life and culture in all the dynamics that characterize the life of the planet. These approaches reexamine our species' history in light of the intensifying awareness of drastic climate change and ongoing mass extinction. To engage this reality, Cambridge Elements in Environmental Humanities builds on the idea of a more hybrid and participatory mode of research and debate, connecting critical and creative fields.

Cambridge Elements Ⲏ

Environmental Humanities

Elements in the Series

Ecosemiotics: The Study of Signs in Changing Ecologies
Timo Maran

The Virus Paradigm: A Planetary Ecology of the Mind
Roberto Marchesini

Ecosemiotic Landscape: A Novel Perspective for the Toolbox of Environmental Humanities
Almo Farina

Wasteocene: Stories from the Global Dump
Marco Armiero

Italo Calvino's Animals: Anthropocene Stories
Serenella Iovino

Deep History, Climate Change, and the Evolution of Human Culture
Louise Westling

Climate Change Literacy
Julia Hoydis, Roman Bartosch and Jens Martin Gurr

Anthroposcreens: Mediating the Climate Unconscious
Julia Leyda

Aging Earth: Senescent Environmentalism for Dystopian Futures
Jacob Jewusiak

Blue Humanities: Storied Waterscapes in the Anthropocene
Serpil Oppermann

Nonhuman Subjects: An Ecology of Earth-Beings
Federico Luisetti

Indigenous Knowledge and Material Histories: The Example of Rubber
Jens Soentgen

A full series listing is available at: www.cambridge.org/EIEH

Printed in the United States
by Baker & Taylor Publisher Services